THE WAY
PEOPLE
LIVE

# Life of a Nazi Soldier

Titles in The Way People Live series include:

Cowboys in the Old West
Games of Ancient Rome
Life Among the Great Plains Indians
Life Among the Ibo Women of Nigeria
Life Among the Indian Fighters
Life Among the Pirates
Life Among the Samurai
Life Among the Vikings
Life During the Black Death
Life During the Crusades
Life During the French Revolution
Life During the Gold Rush
Life During the Great Depression
Life During the Middle Ages
Life During the Renaissance
Life During the Russian Revolution
Life During the Spanish Inquisition
Life in a Japanese American Internment Camp
Life in a Medieval Castle
Life in a Nazi Concentration Camp
Life in Ancient Athens
Life in Ancient China
Life in Ancient Greece
Life in Ancient Rome
Life in a Wild West Show
Life in Charles Dickens's England
Life in the Amazon Rain Forest
Life in the American Colonies
Life in the Elizabethan Theater
Life in the Hitler Youth
Life in the North During the Civil War
Life in the South During the Civil War
Life in the Warsaw Ghetto
Life in War-Torn Bosnia
Life of a Roman Slave
Life of a Slave on a Southern Plantation
Life on a Medieval Pilgrimage
Life on Alcatraz
Life on an African Slave Ship
Life on Ellis Island
Life on the American Frontier
Life on the Oregon Trail
Life on the Underground Railroad
Life Under the Jim Crow Laws
Life of a Roman Soldier

THE WAY PEOPLE LIVE

# Life of a Nazi Soldier

## by Cherese Cartlidge and Charles Clark

Lucent Books, P.O. Box 289011, San Diego, CA 92198-9011

Library of Congress Cataloging-in-Publication Data

Cartlidge, Cherese.
 Life of a Nazi soldier / by Cherese Cartlidge and Charles Clark.
    p. cm. — (The way people live)
Includes bibliographical references and index.
  ISBN 1-56006-484-6 (alk. paper)
  1. Germany. Heer—History—World War, 1939–1945—Juvenile literature.
2. Nazis—Juvenile literature. 3. Germany. Heer—Military life—History—20th
century—Juvenile literature. 4. Soldiers—Germany—History—20th century—
Juvenile literature. [1. Nazis. 2. Soldiers—Germany—History—20th century.
3. Germany—History—1933–1945.] I. Clark, Charles. II. Title. III. Series.
  D757 .C32 2001
  940.54'13'43—dc21

                                                          00-009559

# Contents

**FOREWORD**
Discovering the Humanity in Us All                6

**INTRODUCTION**
Who Were the Nazi Soldiers?                       8

**CHAPTER ONE**
Initiation into Battle                            12

**CHAPTER TWO**
Army of Occupation: Training and Waiting          23

**CHAPTER THREE**
The Eastern Front                                 32

**CHAPTER FOUR**
The Afrika Korps: "To the Last Bullet"            44

**CHAPTER FIVE**
War Crimes                                        54

**CHAPTER SIX**
"Stand and Die": The Defense of
the Fatherland                                    66

**EPILOGUE**
Aftermath                                         78

Notes                                             82
For Further Reading                               85
Works Consulted                                   86
Index                                             90
Picture Credits                                   95
About the Authors                                 96

# Discovering the Humanity in Us All

Books in The Way People Live series focus on groups of people in a wide variety of circumstances, settings, and time periods. Some books focus on different cultural groups, others, on people in a particular historical time period, while others cover people involved in a specific event. Each book emphasizes the daily routines, personal and historical struggles, and achievements of people from all walks of life.

To really understand any culture, it is necessary to strip the mind of the common notions we hold about groups of people. These stereotypes are the archenemies of learning. It does not even matter whether the stereotypes are positive or negative; they are confining and tight. Removing them is a challenge that's not easily met, as anyone who has ever tried it will admit. Ideas that do not fit into the templates we create are unwelcome visitors—ones we would prefer remain quietly in a corner or forgotten room.

The cowboy of the Old West is a good example of such confining roles. The cowboy was courageous, yet soft-spoken. His time (it is always a he, in our template) was spent alternatively saving a rancher's daughter from certain death on a runaway stagecoach, or shooting it out with rustlers. At times, of course, he was likely to get a little crazy in town after a trail drive, but for the most part, he was the epitome of inner strength. It is disconcerting to find out that the cowboy is human, even a bit childish. Can it really be true that cowboys would line up to help the

cook on the trail drive grind coffee, just hoping he would give them a little stick of peppermint candy that came with the coffee shipment? The idea of tough cowboys vying with one another to help "Coosie" (as they called their cooks) for a bit of candy seems silly and out of place.

So is the vision of Eskimos playing video games and watching MTV, living in prefab housing in the Arctic. It just does not fit with what "Eskimo" means. We are far more comfortable with snow igloos and whale blubber, harpoons and kayaks.

Although the cultures dealt with in Lucent's The Way People Live series are often historically and socially well known, the emphasis is on the personal aspects of life. Groups of people, while unquestionably affected by their politics and their governmental structures, are more than those institutions. How do people in a particular time and place educate their children? What do they eat? And how do they build their houses? What kinds of work do they do? What kinds of games do they enjoy? The answers to these questions bring these cultures to life. People's lives are revealed in the particulars and only by knowing the particulars can we understand these cultures' will to survive and their moments of weakness and greatness.

This is not to say that understanding politics does not help to understand a culture. There is no question that the Warsaw ghetto, for example, was a culture that was brought about by the politics and social ideas of Adolf

Hitler and the Third Reich. But the Jews who were crowded together in the ghetto cannot be understood by the Reich's politics. Their life was a day-to-day battle for existence, and the creativity and methods they used to prolong their lives is a vital story of human perseverance that would be denied by focusing only on the institutions of Hitler's Germany. Knowing that children as young as five or six outwitted Nazi guards on a daily basis, that Jewish policemen helped the Germans control the ghetto, that children attended secret schools in the ghetto and even earned diplomas—these are the things that reveal the fabric of life, that can inspire, intrigue, and amaze.

Books in The Way People Live series allow both the casual reader and the student to see humans as victims, heroes, and onlookers. And although humans act in ways that can fill us with feelings of sorrow and revulsion, it is important to remember that "hero," "predator," and "victim" are dangerous terms. Heaping undue pity or praise on people reduces them to objects, and strips them of their humanity.

Seeing the Jews of Warsaw only as victims is to deny their humanity. Seeing them only as they appear in surviving photos, staring at the camera with infinite sadness, is limiting, both to them and to those who want to understand them. To an object of pity, the only appropriate response becomes "Those poor creatures!" and that reduces both the quality of their struggle and the depth of their despair. No one is served by such two-dimensional views of people and their cultures.

With this in mind, The Way People Live series strives to flesh out the traditional, two-dimensional views of people in various cultures and historical circumstances. Using a wide variety of primary quotations—the words not only of the politicians and government leaders, but of the real people whose lives are being examined—each book in the series attempts to show an honest and complete picture of a culture removed from our own by time or space.

By examining cultures in this way, the reader not only will notice the glaring differences from his or her own culture, but also will be struck by the similarities. For indeed, people share common needs—warmth, good company, stability, and affirmation from others. Ultimately, seeing how people really live, or have lived, can only enrich our understanding of ourselves.

# Who Were the Nazi Soldiers?

Adolf Hitler and his armed forces achieved conquests few thought they would even dare. Between 1939 and 1941, the German military overran a huge portion of Europe, from Paris to Moscow, and many Germans felt that they had finally achieved just revenge for the humiliation their country had suffered at the end of World War I. Who were the soldiers who nearly made Hitler's plan to rule Europe a reality?

## Universal Service

Under the Nazi regime, known as the Third Reich (1933–1945), Germany became one of the most militarized societies in history. Even young children underwent military training in the Hitler Youth, membership in which became compulsory for both sexes in 1939. Boys wore uniforms and were taught sports, war games, and Nazi ideology. The girls' organization, called the League of German Girls, taught home economics and courses in matrimony and motherhood. The Labor Service, also a paramilitary organization, was for able-bodied males aged eighteen to twenty-five. Most boys in Germany knew that the normal course of their lives would be membership in the Hitler Youth, then the Labor Service, and then the German armed forces. Virtually all able-bodied men in the Third Reich served in one of three armed, military-style organizations:

- The Wehrmacht, which comprised the army (*Heer*), navy (*Kriegsmarine*), and air force (*Luftwaffe*);

- The SS (*Schutzstaffeln*, meaning "protection squads"), which began as Hitler's bodyguard and expanded to become the most powerful organization in Germany; it was composed of the General SS; the *Waffen*-SS, which was essentially a second army; and the Death's Head SS, which ran the concentration camps;

- The Order Police (*Ordnungpolizei*), which brought all local and regional police forces under the direct control of the Nazi regime.

The SS and the Order Police were given military training, and in many cases they were uniformed, armed, barracked, and deployed like the regular army. Their legitimate functions were much the same as military police today, but they also engaged in the political repression of German citizens and in the persecution and murder of Jews and other minorities. Both the SS and the Order Police could operate anywhere they were assigned in Germany and in conquered countries, and they were an integral part of military operations.

Membership in the SS was open to members of the Nazi Party who could meet strict physical and ideological requirements. Loyalty to Hitler and to the ideals of the Nazi regime were absolute requirements. The overriding idea of the Nazi regime was to create a perfect Germanic race that would rule Europe, achieved in part by killing everyone defined by the regime as less than perfect: the disabled, the mentally ill, homosexuals, and anyone who was not purely or mostly German—including Jews, Slavs, and Gypsies. The Nazis killed at least 6 million noncombatants, that is, people who were not soldiers, before and during the war. This figure is probably low, however, because they deliberately killed many civilians in violation of international law, especially on the eastern front, and the numbers are lost in the fog of battle.

## Propaganda

Propaganda helped to create a culture in which German soldiers were willing to commit themselves to the destruction of entire races of people. Propaganda about the superiority of the Aryan race and the inferiority of the Jews dominated the German education system. Despite this, not all German soldiers were Nazis, as former artillery officer Siegfried Knappe explains in his memoir, *Soldat:* "Those of us who were soldiers in the German Army during World War II were young men fighting for their country. We were not 'Nazi' soldiers; we were just German soldiers."[1]

A major objective of Nazi propaganda was to promote the goal of uniting all those in Europe who were ethnically German in a so-called Greater Germany (*Grossdeutschland*). Protecting and assimilating ethnic Germans in other countries was Germany's principal justification for taking over Austria and the Sudetenland area of Czechoslovakia in 1938. Because of this Greater Germany policy, not all Nazi soldiers were German; many were

*A familiar scene in World War II: a German infantryman throwing the "potato masher" hand grenade.*

recruited from elsewhere in Europe, especially to become members of the *Waffen*-SS. In addition, men in some areas conquered by the Nazis were forced into the German army. For example, in the Alsace-Lorraine region of France, forty thousand men were conscripted into the German armed forces.

## The New Wehrmacht

Nazi ideology emphasized the unity and equality of the German people, a belief clearly reflected in the army. Before the Nazis came to power, the officer corps of the army had been composed almost entirely of relatively wealthy and educated men, while the enlisted ranks were filled with working-class men. The Nazis, however, opened the officer corps to anyone who showed leadership ability, and they taught that all soldiers should take responsibility for the successful outcome of each mission. This produced a leadership structure that the men respected and were loyal to. According to former German soldier Hans Woltersdorf, "The real background to our elite combat record [was] the special leadership principle. . . . The necessary qualification for an officer's career was not the high school diploma but exemplary ability, the true authority. Everyone who led a unit had to be the best man in his unit as well; not the uniform . . . but example made the leader."[2]

## The Treaty of Versailles

In *The Road to War: The Origins of World War II*, Richard Overy and Andrew Wheatcroft write about the sense of injustice and betrayal many Germans felt after learning of the terms of the Versailles treaty, signed in April 1919, that officially ended World War I.

"The reality faced by the German delegation in France exceeded even the most pessimistic expectations. The envoys were placed in an isolated hotel surrounded by barbed wire. They were brought to the conference as a defeated and guilty enemy. The Allied delegates sat; the Germans were made to stand. 'The hour has struck,' said Georges Clemenceau, head of the French delegation, 'for the weighty settlement of our account.' It was an account no German could believe. Germany was to be almost completely disarmed, confined to a 100,000 man army for internal police responsibilities, denied the use of tanks, warplanes and submarines, the great German General Staff disbanded. The German . . . colonies were taken over by the newly formed League of Nations. . . . One-eighth of German territory was distributed to France and Belgium in the west, Denmark in the north and Poland and Czechoslovakia in the east. The Polish settlement was a bitter blow. The Allies agreed to allow Poland a 'corridor' of territory to the sea carved out of West Prussia, . . . leaving a vulnerable rump of East Prussia surrounded by Polish territory. . . . The Rhineland was permanently demilitarized. The final humiliation was the Allied insistence that Germany admit its war guilt formally, . . . and that having done so the German government should undertake to pay in reparation . . . 132 billion gold marks; the schedule of payments drawn up in 1921 would have burdened the German economy until 1988."

## For Führer, Folk, and Fatherland

Whether they were citizens of Germany or of one of the occupied countries, and whether they were members of the Nazi Party, made little difference—soldiers of the Third Reich shared an excitement over and commitment to a new era for Europe with the German people as the undisputed rulers of the continent. Many thought that Adolf Hitler, their führer, or leader, was the savior of Germany and the greatest military commander in history. They thought that the German people (the Folk, or in German, *Volk*) were superior to all others and could accomplish anything. And they felt that Germany, the Fatherland, should dominate Europe.

In the 1930s, few outside of Germany understood the source of Nazi power and the danger it posed, and so the rest of Europe and the United States were unprepared for war. But as Robert Boothby, an adviser to British prime minister Winston Churchill, wrote in March 1940, the Nazis were not merely a political party but a *"movement— young, virile, dynamic, and violent—which is advancing irresistibly to overthrow a decaying old world. . . . [I]t is the source of the Nazi strength and power."*[3] German paratrooper Martin Pöppel expressed the feelings of many German soldiers when he wrote, "We were uncritically enthusiastic, proud to be alive in times we regarded as heroic."[4]

# 1 Initiation into Battle

One provision of the Treaty of Versailles, which officially ended World War I (1914–1918), was that the defeated Germany could have a standing army of no more than one hundred thousand men. Many Germans thought this provision of the treaty unfair because it left their country vulnerable to invasion. The German economy had been crippled by another aspect of the treaty known as reparations, which were payments Germany was forced to make to its former enemies. In addition, the global economic depression had left many Germans unemployed.

For all these reasons, in the 1930s many young German men were eager to join the army. The politician who called the loudest for an expansion of the army was Adolf Hitler, leader of the National Socialist German Workers' Party—the Nazis. Hitler became chancellor of Germany in January 1933. Over the next eighteen months he and the Nazi Party eliminated freedom of the press, banned opposing political parties, appointed party members to head all important state and national government agencies, and jailed anyone who spoke out against the Nazi regime. With political opposition effectively silenced, Hitler began to defy the terms of the Versailles treaty. Hitler sensed that the other countries of Europe dreaded another military confrontation with Germany and so would take no action against him. In 1934, Hitler decreed that Germany would increase its army to three hundred thousand, three times what the treaty allowed. Over one hundred thou-

sand men volunteered that year alone. The following year, Hitler reintroduced a military draft and announced a plan for an army of five hundred thousand men. By September 1, 1939, when Germany invaded Poland and started World War II, its army numbered 3.7 million.

## Military Training

Most men entering the German army had been through rigorous training in the Hitler Youth and Reich Labor Service, but the intensity of army training was even greater. German recruits were told over and over that "sweat saves blood." In other words, the harder they trained before battle, the better their chances of survival. German training was intense, realistic, nearly continuous, and often cruel by modern standards. Former infantryman Guy Sajer says that on his first day of training with the *Grossdeutschland* Division, he and his unit were shown as well as told what would be required of them by their commander, Captain Fink:

> Simply maintaining a decent level of morale and knowing how to handle a weapon will no longer be enough. You will also require a very great deal of courage, of perseverance and endurance, and of resistance in any situation. . . . We need men, and not pitiful specimens like you. I must warn you that everything here

is hard, nothing is forgiven, and that everyone in consequence must have quick reflexes. . . .

"Attention!" he shouted. "Down on the ground, and full length!"

Without a moment's hesitation, we were all stretched out on the sandy soil. Then Captain Fink [who weighed over two hundred pounds] stepped forward and . . . walked across the human ground, continuing his speech as his boots . . . trampled the paralyzed bodies of our section. His heels calmly crushed down on a back, a hip, a head, a hand—but no one moved.[5]

## Preparing for War

In the 1920s and 1930s, Germany was a deeply divided country. While some Germans wanted peace with neighboring countries, many politicians and ordinary citizens were angered by the humiliations of the Versailles treaty and fearful that Germany would be attacked and conquered. They especially feared the Soviet Union but also distrusted France, neighbors whose borders with Germany were historically contested. Hitler and the Nazis used these fears to justify a military buildup that was enthusiastically supported by both current soldiers and new recruits.

The rationale for German rearmament was stated most clearly by one of Hitler's favorite

*Adolf Hitler addresses the Hitler Youth during a rally in 1934.*

The development of combat tanks began in World War I, but several European nations were slow to realize the decisive role tanks could play in modern warfare. Though the French had some modern tanks, most of them were used to support infantry units, which meant that the tanks could advance no faster than a soldier could walk. In February 1935, however, Adolf Hitler saw a demonstration of tanks organized by General Heinz Guderian at a secret testing ground at Kummersdorf, south of Berlin. Hitler was impressed by the capabilities of the tanks and by Guderian's ideas for how to use them. Hitler reportedly said, "That's what I need. That's what I want to have," and soon tanks became central to the Nazi war machine.

The first German tank, the Panzer I, was about fifteen feet long, weighed less than six tons, carried two crew members, was lightly armored, and had only two machine guns. It was useless in battle but taught German designers many valuable lessons. The Panzer II, developed in 1937, weighed ten tons and employed a converted twenty-millimeter anti-aircraft gun. Though an improvement over the Panzer I, it was still small compared to the eighty-one-ton French Char 3c. The Germans hoped to compensate for this lack of bulk by making tanks that were faster, and by making more of them—they built fourteen hundred Panzer IIs.

In the invasions of Poland and France, the Germans used Panzer IIs for many tasks but relied on the larger and better-armed Panzer III and IV models for battle situations. The Panzer III weighed twenty-two tons and had a fifty-millimeter gun. The Panzer IV weighed twenty-six tons and had a seventy-five-millimeter gun. However, early in the war the Germans were not able to make as many of

*The German army's first tank, the Panzer I, passes Adolf Hitler at a review before the start of World War II.*

these tanks as they needed. Len Deighton explains the situation in his book *Blitzkrieg*:

"While the [Panzer] I and II were too flimsy and primitive, the [Panzer] III and IV designs overcompensated for these failings. They were complex machines that gave too many problems to the engineering department and often had to go back to the factories for repairs. . . . Comfortable to ride in, they were almost luxurious in design, though the armament did not provide enough hitting power to justify the high unit cost. Indeed, each machine was handmade. . . .

The scarcity of the [Panzer] IIIs and IVs makes it now seem very doubtful whether any attack against France in 1940 would have been contemplated without the resources the Germans gained [when they invaded] Czechoslovakia. . . . Discounting lightweight German training tanks, no less than one third of the German armor used against France originated in Czech factories."

soldiers, General Heinz Guderian. In his book *Achtung-Panzer!*, written in 1937, Guderian says that all the nations of Europe were preparing for war, and any country that did not arm itself would be attacked; that though other countries had mountain ranges and oceans to protect them from invasion, Germany did not; that other countries had either vast resources such as oil, minerals, and population or colonies to supply these resources, but Germany did not. Therefore, Germany was threatened, but it was too small to fight a long war. Guderian concluded that "nations [like Germany] who are unable to tolerate a long period of hostilities, with all its attendant economic privations . . . have been forced to consider what means may best . . . bring an armed conflict to a rapid and tolerable end."[6]

In other words, German commanders felt compelled to adopt a strategy for fighting a brief, intense war and forcing an acceptable peace. That strategy came to be known as blitzkrieg, a German term meaning "lightning war."

## Blitzkrieg

All the military training the young men of Germany went through in the late 1930s was designed to prepare them for blitzkrieg. General Guderian planned and supervised the building of the proper equipment (such as tanks) and the training of Nazi soldiers to wage blitzkrieg. Following Guderian's plan, the *Luftwaffe* (the German air force) would be deployed first to bomb the enemy's air force and other strategic installations. Then, the tanks would roll in. The mechanized forces of the Third Reich had the option of either encircling the enemy—the old but still effective way of winning a battle—or fighting through enemy lines to reach strategic objectives such as bridges, ports, and major cities.

By the time World War II began in 1939, the airplanes, tanks, trucks, and radio communications of the German army were among the best in the world, and they were organized for maximum effectiveness. The French army had more tanks than the Germans (three thousand to the Germans' twenty-four hundred), but the French spread theirs throughout the army, with tanks often accompanying infantry units that still moved by foot and horseback. The Germans, on the other hand, kept their tanks together and supported them with motorized artillery and cargo trucks. The Germans also made sure that, except in bad weather, their air force would be able to clear the way for the tanks. The Germans' Messerschmitt 109, a fighter, and Junkers 87 or Stuka, a dive-bomber, were perfectly matched to the strategy of blitzkrieg. They could attack swiftly and without warning to destroy enemy airfields and harass supply and troop columns.

This technical and organizational superiority made it possible for the Nazi army to move more quickly and respond more effectively than their opponents to changes in battlefield circumstances. According to Wehrmacht officer Alexander Stahlberg, in some ways blitzkrieg was like the methods of ancient armies, "fighting where the opportunity offered, marching where it seemed possible to wring some advantage from movement, retaining the initiative, waging a mobile war according to the classical models of world history."[7]

Hans Luck was a tank officer who fought under Erwin Rommel, perhaps the most famous German general of World War II. According to Luck, Rommel's orders in the invasion of France summed up the role of the mechanized forces in blitzkrieg: "Keep going, don't look to left or right, only forward. I'll cover your flanks if necessary. The enemy is confused; we must take advantage of it."[8]

## Surprise and Speed

An important element of blitzkrieg was surprise. Often even German soldiers themselves were unsure of their mission until the last moment. Hans Luck writes of his tank division:

> Officially we were to take part in "grand maneuvers under combat conditions." Although live ammunition was being carried, we were issued only blanks.... On our eastward march we went through the Sudetenland and continued past Prague in the direction of the Reich frontier in the region of Gleiwitz [Poland]. Local people greeted us everywhere with flowers and drinks.
>
> "Are you going to Poland?" we were asked.
>
> "Of course not," we replied, "we're going on maneuvers."[9]

The rationale for blitzkrieg, the reason the Germans developed it in the first place, was that the Nazi war machine was not well suited for a long war. Oil and fuel shortages were a problem in every campaign and worsened as the war dragged on. Another reason Germany needed quick victories was the limitations of their horse-drawn supply vehicles. The Nazis needed to gain control of a country's railheads so they could supply their troops.

The superbly conditioned German infantry troops were able to march up to forty miles a day in the Polish campaign. Each man carried a Mauser rifle weighing about eleven pounds, sixty rounds of ammunition, two hand grenades, a gas mask, a canteen and mess kit, an entrenching tool, and a rucksack. Using blitzkrieg

methods, German armies swept through Europe, conquering country after country with astonishing speed. Poland was defeated in only twenty-seven days; Norway in twenty-eight days; Denmark in one day; the Netherlands in five days; Belgium in eighteen days; and France, with the largest army and second-largest navy in Europe, in forty-two days.

## First Battle: The Polish Campaign

For many German soldiers, their first battle came during the invasion of Poland in September 1939. Many of them later wrote that no matter how much training they had received, actual battle was a shock, full of danger, noise, horror, and the unexpected. The bullets and shells were real, aimed at them, and in the confusion and panic of battle anything could happen. Many German soldiers became unnerved during their first battle. General Heinz Guderian wrote of his arrival at one of the first battlefields in Poland:

> There was a thick ground mist at first which prevented the air force from giving us any support. . . . Unfortunately the heavy artillery of the 3rd Panzer Division felt itself compelled to fire into the mist, despite having received precise orders not to do so. The first shell landed 50 yards ahead of my command vehicle, the second 50 yards behind it. I reckoned that the next one was bound to be a direct hit and ordered my driver to turn about and drive off. The unaccustomed noise had made him nervous, however, and he drove straight into a ditch at full speed. . . . This marked the end of my drive. I . . . procured myself a fresh vehicle and had a word with the over-eager artillerymen.[10]

In contrast to Guderian's experience, Captain Hans Luck's reconnaissance regiment, a group that searched out enemy positions, encountered no Polish troops until late the same evening. This gave them the feeling of still being on maneuvers during the daylight hours, but Luck describes how he and his men were confronted that night by the grim realities of war:

> In front of us lay an open, rising tract of land. . . . Here the Poles had set up a line of resistance on a hill, and opened a heavy fire from machine guns and mortars. Shell splinters hissed through the trees. Branches broke off and fell on our heads.

*German troops roll through Poland in September 1939.*

. . . We had often practiced under combat conditions, of course, and had been able thereby to get used to the firing and the landing of artillery shells, as well as the sharp hammering of machine-guns. But that had always been at a safe distance or from bunkers under cover.

Now, we were directly exposed to enemy fire. We could find no cover, nor could we dig ourselves in, since we were supposed to attack. We formed up for the assault. . . .

Suddenly a round of machine-gun fire hit Private Uhl, not far from me. He was dead at once. He was the first casualty in my company, and many of my men saw it. Now we were all afraid. Which of us would be the next? This was no longer a maneuver; it was war.[11]

## Between Campaigns: The *Sitzkrieg*

In the blitzkrieg campaigns in Poland and western Europe, the actual fighting often only took a few days. Next the German troops would find housing, generally by taking over hotels and other large facilities and in some cases by evicting people from their houses. They also set up governments of occupation, taking over the running of the countries, and arrested or executed anyone who attempted armed resistance.

A big part of blitzkrieg was getting ready for the next fight. After each campaign, most German soldiers were put to work moving weapons and supplies to strategic locations and continuing to train. The longest period of waiting and preparing for battle came after the invasion of Poland. Britain and France

*German shock troops prepare an assault on an enemy position.*

declared war on Germany on September 3, 1939. The Germans expected a British-French invasion and immediately sent troops to fortify Germany's western borders, but there was no fighting until the following spring. Among frontline German troops this period became known as the *Sitzkrieg,* or "sitting war."

In his memoir *Soldat,* artillery officer Siegfried Knappe describes some of his duties during the *Sitzkrieg*—his battalion left for western Germany the day after Britain and France declared war on his country. Knappe was part of a new artillery battalion, using reserves who had been called up and horses that had been appropriated from civilian owners. When Knappe's battalion arrived in western Germany, they still expected an invasion by French and British troops across Germany's border with Luxembourg. Their first step in defending their frontier was to dig in. Knappe describes this process in his memoir:

About five kilometers east of the Luxembourg border . . . in a heavily wooded sector . . . Hauptmann Wimmer [the battery commander] issued orders to set the guns into firing position, pointed toward the border, and to camouflage them. We ordered . . . telephone lines laid between the forward observation post and the gun positions. . . . We established a guarded perimeter area and immediately began digging in.

The smell of freshly dug earth mingled with the natural odor of the decaying leaves of the forest in the warm September afternoon. Soon the odor of sweating bodies was added to the others. After digging foxholes, the men began building bunkers. . . . The men cut down small trees . . . trimmed the limbs off the trees, stood the trunks on end, side by side, and chinked between them with mud. . . . The men rigged bunks with pole frames for themselves . . . seven or eight men to a bunker. . . .

Of course, the guns and the bunkers were all camouflaged so they could not be detected from the air.[12]

## Holidays and Leisure Time

During the *Sitzkrieg*, many German soldiers went home for the holidays. According to Knappe, half the men in his battalion got five days' leave around Christmas and the other half got five days around New Year's Day. In December 1939, Karl Fuchs wrote to his mother that "our entire unit will celebrate Christmas together. Of course, we intend to buy a small Christmas tree. This will be my first Christmas Eve in the military. Who knows how many others will follow! I guess it doesn't matter. Our duty is to defend our Fatherland."[13]

Knappe's battery was stationed at the small village of Leitzkau, Germany, beginning in January 1940. He writes that the "winter weather was very cold, but the men were dressed for it. We had to break the ice to water the horses on most days, and . . . the men could ice-skate in their free time without danger of breaking through the ice."[14]

## The Invasion of France

Everyone knew the *Sitzkrieg* could not last indefinitely. It ended on May 10, 1940, when German forces invaded Holland and Belgium. The blitzkrieg attack advanced rapidly toward its goal of destroying the Allied armies and gaining control of a substantial portion of France, especially the coast along the English Channel. Though the soldiers had trained for years in blitzkrieg tactics, according to Knappe,

the success of the German army surprised even the Germans. His group relied on horses and so moved more slowly than the tank divisions, which accomplished their mission quickly.

## Guderian's Victory Message

General Heinz Guderian spent much of his career developing the Wehrmacht's ability to wage blitzkrieg, and in the invasion of France his abilities both as a planner and as a field commander were proven. In his book *Panzer Leader*, he includes his message to his troops following the invasion.

"For seventeen days we have been fighting in Belgium and France. . . . You have thrust through the Belgian fortifications, forced a passage of the Meuse [River], broken the Maginot Line extension in the memorable Battle of Sedan, captured the important heights at Stonne and then, without halt, fought your way through St. Quentin and Péronne to the lower Somme [River] at Amiens and Abbéville. You have set the crown on your achievements by the capture of the Channel Coast and of the sea fortresses at Boulogne and Calais.

I asked you to go without sleep for 48 hours. You have gone for 17 days. I compelled you to accept risks. . . . You never faltered. . . . You carried out every order with devotion.

Germany is proud of her Panzer Divisions and I am happy to be your commander.

We remember our fallen comrades with honour and respect, sure in the knowledge that their sacrifice was not in vain.

Now we arm ourselves for new deeds.

For Germany and our leader, Adolf Hitler!"

In his memoir *Soldat*, German artillery officer Siegfried Knappe describes his first experience with the realities of war during the invasion of France.

"We were familiar with the dust and the smells of burned powder and gasoline from maneuvers, but this was our first exposure to the smell of death. Dead cattle and other livestock were everywhere, the victims of bullets, mortars, artillery shells, and bombs. Their bloating carcasses lay in the fields with their legs sticking up. I learned that the smell of rotting flesh, dust, burned powder, smoke, and gasoline was the smell of combat. This was my first exposure to it, but it was an odor that was to become all too familiar to me during the next five years.

My first sight of a dead soldier was an unexpected shock. We had been trained to deliver death quickly and efficiently, and we knew that in war people get killed. But 'knowing' it intellectually was entirely different from seeing and experiencing it. We had known officers from our own regiment who had been killed in Poland, of course, and we felt a sense of loss—but the word 'killed' still had a clinical connotation about it compared to its meaning when you saw lying on the ground before you a bloodied, mutilated, foul-smelling corpse that had previously been a vital, living human being. Now the former human being was just a gruesome, lifeless thing on the ground.

The first dead soldiers I saw were French Moroccans. They had been killed in a cemetery, and they lay where they had fallen, their limbs in grotesque positions, their eyes and mouths open. The experience was impossible to forget. This was what we were doing to people and what they were doing to us. It was devastating to realize that this was what we had to look forward to every day, day after day, until the war was over. From that moment on, death hovered near us wherever we went."

*Dead German soldiers await burial.*

Knappe's division was part of a large force preparing to break through the French defenses on the Somme River and then move on to take Paris. Knappe describes what it was like when the fighting began:

It was here that we fired our first round of the war and experienced our first direct combat. In the afternoon . . . the French attacked us with a heavy artillery barrage. The sound of the exploding artillery shells was nerve-wracking at first, but I was surprised at how quickly I got used to it. . . . Our world was filled with explosions, the smell of burned powder, trembling earth, and frenzied activity. Our guncrews, pumped full of adrenaline by fear and excitement, hurled shell after shell at the French. When it was over, we were almost in a daze—from exhaustion, from excitement, and from the sudden silence following the incredible roar of combat. We actually felt light-headed.[15]

As his division drove deep into France, Alexander Stahlberg saw his first battle and was especially impressed with the capabilities of the *Luftwaffe*. He writes that

above us . . . there were fierce dogfights between German and Allied pilots. We followed them with our binoculars, admiring the courage with which the adversaries, whether Allied or German, hurled themselves at each other. Then, in the distance, we saw our new dive bombers in action for the first time. Engines howling, they plummeted like birds of prey towards their targets on the ground, pulling out at the last moment as they released their bombs. Everything we saw, on the ground and in the air, seemed to add up to great superiority on our side. On we rolled, always to the West.[16]

## Coping with the Stress of Battle

Though the early campaigns in Poland and western Europe were easy victories for the German armed forces, individual soldiers had to deal with all the frights, fears, and shocks of battle. They coped in a variety of ways. Knappe and his men expected combat at any moment, even during the relatively uneventful months of the *Sitzkrieg*. They coped with this constant uncertainty by throwing themselves into training, at least partly to distract themselves from thinking about what might happen in battle. Knappe writes that "the stress of not knowing when we might be attacked was incentive enough to drive the men to work hard to become an effective fighting unit. We had trained for combat, and with a confidence born of youth and innocence, I did not consciously think of the possibility of dying or being mutilated in combat."[17]

When the fighting actually began, however, the nearness of death could no longer be denied. Knappe explains that he found "combat to be both exhilarating and frightening. It was exhilarating because while the noise and action were going on we lived in a high state of excitement. It was frightening because at any moment an exploding shell could blast us into eternity. No one could know one minute whether he would be alive the next."[18]

Hans Luck writes about his mindset for survival and how, at the end of the French campaign, he and his men coped with grief for those fallen in combat, worries about their families at home, and feelings about having taken human lives:

Probably every soldier finds out in the course of a war that he can only bear the "having to kill" and "being killed" over long periods if he adopts the maxims of the Stoics: learn to endure all things with equanimity. He can only do this if he builds up an immune system of his own against the feelings of fear and sympathy and probably, to a certain degree, even against matters of ethics, morals, and conscience. He cannot afford to question the whys and wherefores of the things that happen around him and in which he, himself, has a part. . . . He learns . . . to suppress images of horror, to distance himself from his neighbor in order to remain capable of rational action. If he manages to do this, his chances of survival increase.[19]

In the early days of World War II, the soldiers of Nazi Germany were initiated into battle on a wave of victories that stunned the world. Their level of ideological indoctrination, physical training, and strategic readiness for the realities of the modern battlefield were unprecedented and led directly to their triumphs. But their very success would eventually be their undoing as they conquered more and more territory that they were unable to occupy and hold.

# Army of Occupation: Training and Waiting

During World War II, Germany conquered and occupied most of Europe: Poland, Czechoslovakia, Norway, Denmark, the Netherlands, Belgium, Luxembourg, France, Greece, Crete, Italy, Hungary, Yugoslavia, and the Soviet Union. The experience of Nazi soldiers varied greatly depending on the degree of cooperation or resistance in the conquered country and the stage of the war. In relating to the local populations, soldiers were variously conquerors, tourists, policemen, or bureaucrats; they humiliated the local people and were humiliated in return; they were the targets of resistance fighters and instruments of revenge. But friendships and even romances also developed between German soldiers and the people whose countries they had conquered. The soldiers' experience in France, the largest and most prosperous of the occupied countries, illustrates many aspects of life for the German army in occupied countries.

## Soldier-Sightseers

Weary from the brief but intense fighting of the recent blitzkrieg, most German soldiers in France took time to relax once the hostilities ended. For many of these young men, the war was the first time they had traveled outside Germany. France was a foreign country, a new and exciting place to explore. Many soldiers had brought their cameras, and in the early weeks of the occupation they behaved like tourists, taking in such sights as the Tomb of the Unknown Soldier and the Louvre museum in Paris. In his memoir, artillery officer Siegfried Knappe describes his visit to Paris in September 1940: "I stayed there a couple of days to enjoy the famous city. I went to the opera and I visited the Panthéon, Notre-Dame, the Arc de Triomphe, the Champs-Élysées, and even *climbed* the Eiffel Tower. While I was in Paris, I reveled in the architecture of the beautiful city and its cultural wealth."[20]

German soldiers took advantage of the amenities France had to offer—luxuries they

*A sight-seeing German soldier takes pictures after the fall of France.*

## Proud German Sons and Daughters

As the Wehrmacht advanced swiftly through France, many German soldiers were proud of their success and regarded their fight as heroic. Officer candidate Karl Fuchs was stationed at Bamberg Army Base in Germany at this time. On May 19 Fuchs wrote to Mädi, his bride of three weeks.

"The whole base is excited. . . . The German army is before the gates of Paris! It is wonderful what our soldiers are achieving! It is as if the old Teutonic spirit and the old strength of our forefathers are with them. Friedrich Barbarossa [king of Germany, 1155–1190] has arisen! He is with us in our fight against our archenemy. He leads us on to greater victories and soon to peace. And this Friedrich Barbarossa is none other than our Führer Adolf Hitler.

Today we are proud. We can be proud to be German sons and daughters. . . . Our love for each other is at the same time a love for our 'Volk' [the German people] and nothing should be more important to us than to devote our entire strength and all our efforts for this magnificent 'Volk.' If this is achieved, the two of us will also be able to live in peace."

---

had had to do without during the blitzkrieg. Hans Luck's 7th Panzer Division was stationed briefly at the French seaside resort of Arcachon. He writes, "There among the dunes I set up my headquarters in one of the pretty summer villas. For a few days we enjoyed bathing in the sea, fresh oysters . . . and the delicious dry white wine."[21]

## The Occupation of France

Occupying a country presented its own set of problems for the Nazis. After their quick conquest of France, they found themselves faced with administering the country. In 1940 a central French collaborationist government had been established in Vichy, in central France. Some German officers contacted old friends or local officials to ask for help in setting up local occupation administrations. Essential services such as police, railways, mining, and postal services continued to operate with French officials under strict German control. German sentries stood guard at public buildings, road-ways, borders, and demarcation lines, and soldiers were posted along frontiers.

The fighting in France ended with the armistice, but many German soldiers continued to train for combat. They trained in preparation for Operation Sea Lion, the planned invasion of England, and for combat in Russia. They also anticipated an invasion of the European continent by England and the United States to reclaim the countries the Germans had just conquered. Many soldiers, including Karl Fuchs, found the constant training dull and monotonous. Fuchs wrote to his father, asking, "What is there to gain from the constant drill in the courtyard, from superiors always screaming 'about face' and the like? With every passing day, the activity here resembles basic training more and more."[22] Martin Pöppel, a paratrooper and machine gunner who was stationed in southern France during the occupation, describes his training: "For weeks now there have been daily exercises to prepare against enemy operations by land and air. . . . Over and over again, weapons containers are packed at top speed and embarkation exercises perfected. Scarcely a night goes by without us being turfed from our beds to improve our combat readiness."[23]

## Room and Board

Food in occupied countries was requisitioned for soldiers or sent to Germany. Food was rationed for French civilians, but not for the German occupiers in France: In some places, soldiers found themselves eating better than they had in their homeland. Knappe observes:

The French people in Candé were living quite well, considerably better than the German population in big cities. We lived better in Candé than I had at home on convalescent leave. In Germany, every-

thing was rationed—food, clothing, gasoline, etc. But in Candé, we could go to restaurants and get anything we wanted without ration cards. We could buy any food we wanted from local farmers.[24]

Pöppel elaborates on how well he and fellow soldiers ate while they were stationed in Saint Sever, France, in 1942: "There's still an abundance of food here, the fried potatoes swimming in fat, the butter spread centimeters thick and gorgeous fruit on the bedside table—peaches, and grapes by the pound. As our saying goes, in France you can live like a god."[25]

Hotels, villas, and private homes were requisitioned for office space and living quarters. In some cases, monasteries or country chalets (cottages) were requisitioned as vacation sites

*German soldiers enjoy a meal at a French restaurant in the Alsace-Lorraine region during the German occupation of France.*

for officers. While he was stationed in Bordeaux, Luck was billeted at the Grand Hotel. He and his men took their meals on the terrace of the hotel. As Luck writes in his memoirs, he was "somewhat embarrassed to think that other guests had probably been forced to vacate their rooms on our behalf. . . . We met with hostile looks from many of the guests. I felt somewhat ill at ease. Yet, it was pleasant to sit on the terrace."[26]

Claire Chevrillon was a Frenchwoman who lived in occupied Paris. Her parents' home was requisitioned to house eighty members of the *Luftwaffe*. A friend wrote to her in 1940: "We walked by your house, and there, up on the roof, were quite a few [German] men, their chests bare, sunbathing. They were singing at the top of their lungs to a loud record. When we passed by again later, these gentlemen were having tea in the dining room, on one of your beautiful tablecloths."[27]

A soldier's living conditions depended on his assignment and could vary greatly over the course of the war. As Pöppel writes, "In normal conditions we're housed very comfortably in French villas, but when we're put on standby by the Division and told to maintain combat readiness, then we have to pitch camp in the old barracks."[28]

## Off-Duty Activities

Many Nazi soldiers went home for their vacation days, furloughs, and holidays. Others vacationed in neutral Switzerland, the French

## Hitler in Paris

After the fall of France, German soldiers celebrated their victory with daily ceremonial marches in Paris, goose stepping triumphantly down the Avenue des Champs-Élysées. This enthusiasm was clearly shared by Adolf Hitler. William L. Shirer, an American reporter, was present when Hitler came to Paris on June 25, 1940, as its new ruler. Shirer's description of the scene as Hitler was about to meet with French officials to dictate the terms of peace is quoted in *Reporting World War II: American Journalism, 1938–1944:*

"I saw the Führer stop [and] observe the Reich flags with their big Swastikas in the centre. Then he strode slowly towards us. . . . I observed his face. It was grave, solemn, yet brimming with revenge. There was also in it, as in his springy step, a note of the triumphant conqueror, the defier of the world. There was something else, difficult to describe, in his expression, a sort of scornful, inner joy at being present at this great reversal of fate—a reversal he himself had wrought."

*Adolf Hitler celebrates the fall of France by posing for photographers at the Eiffel Tower in June 1940.*

seaside, or went skiing in the Austrian Alps. Knappe writes of his off-duty time, "Once each month, Major Raake hosted a dinner for all the officers under his command. Some of us also occasionally went pheasant hunting along the Loire River, using some of the shotguns we had confiscated from the local population."[29]

Paris was a favorite destination for off-duty relaxation. Members of the Wehrmacht were entitled to free fare on trains, and the subway in Paris was usually packed with Germans. The German mark, worth only six francs in 1939, was decreed by German authorities to be worth twenty francs in 1940. With such a favorable exchange rate, soldiers flocked to French shops to buy up items unobtainable in Germany, such as clothing, wine, perfume, and silk stockings for wives and girlfriends.

A favorite pastime for French civilians and German soldiers alike was the horse races. At racetracks like Auteuil and Longchamp, outside Paris, the stands were reserved for Germans. Likewise, many restaurants and nightclubs were reserved for Germans. Maxim's, a famous Paris restaurant, had been requisitioned by the Nazis and was run by a Berlin restaurateur named Otto Horcher. Restaurants and nightclubs were expensive, but with their high pay German soldiers could afford such luxury items as meat, which was rationed for civilians, and champagne and other wines.

Soldiers also enjoyed going to the opera and the theater. At a *Soldatenkino* (soldier's theater), where civilians were forbidden, members of the Wehrmacht could watch German films. Plays by William Shakespeare, Henrik Ibsen, and George Bernard Shaw were also staged in Paris during the war.

A large number of soldiers, including Fuchs and Knappe, went home on furloughs to get married. Soldiers who wanted to get married had to obtain special permission from the adjutant-general of the Wehrmacht

High Command as well as their divisional commander. Proof of Aryan descent, three character testimonials, and a medical certificate were also required of the bride-to-be. Wedding plans had to be flexible because soldiers' furloughs frequently were cancelled on the grounds of military necessity. When this happened to Knappe just before he was ready to leave for his wedding, he was unable to notify his family or fiancée in Germany because of military secrecy. Ten days later, when the restriction on furloughs was lifted, he went home for a rescheduled wedding.

## Contact with Civilians

Military regulations also specified how German soldiers were to treat French civilians. In her memoir *Code Name Christiane Clouet: A Woman in the French Resistance*, Claire Chevrillon describes the general behavior of German soldiers in occupied France:

> The German soldiers were under orders to be polite, and so they were. . . . The Germans kept themselves on a short leash in Brittany. Two months earlier in Poland they had behaved quite differently. In Port-Blanc [France] they did everything they could to curry favor. They avoided going into homes, or when they had to, did it deferentially. They gave candy to the children. In shops or farms they paid a bit more than the going rate for whatever they bought. This was easy for them because the authorities had decreed the mark to be worth twenty francs, so that "Fritz" was rich and could send his family in Germany things now inaccessible to the French. The message the Germans wanted to get across was on posters they'd put up all over town showing a

*A German soldier buys goods at a French market. It was not uncommon for soldiers to fraternize openly with the French during the four years of occupation.*

Nazi soldier carrying a toddler. The caption read: "Put your trust in German soldiers."[30]

## Fraternization

The Nazi occupation of France lasted four years. During that time, it was inevitable that some degree of fraternization—friendly association—between German soldiers and French civilians would occur. Despite the fact that they had invaded and conquered France, many Germans who occupied the country had old friends or even relatives in the country. New friendships were also formed as day-to-day life in occupied France continued for soldiers and civilians alike. It was not uncommon for soldiers to fraternize openly with

Frenchwomen, dining or drinking together in restaurants and nightclubs. Many soldiers even had French girlfriends or wives. In 1943, eighty-five thousand illegitimate children were born as the result of relationships between German soldiers and Frenchwomen.

French people who thought fraternization was the same as collaboration—willing assistance of the Nazis—reacted harshly. French resistance fighters shaved the heads of women who had slept with Germans to mark them as collaborators. Other French people were murdered by their fellow citizens in retaliation for their relationships with the enemy occupiers, usually because they were suspected of giving the Germans information about resistance activities.

German soldiers had to take these things into account when contemplating taking up old friendships—or creating new ones—in

France. Luck was on friendly terms with the elderly female owner of a local establishment in Bordeaux, where he and his men were treated to champagne whenever they visited. He writes in his memoirs, "I hope this charming woman did not have to suffer later as a *collaborateuse*."[31]

## Resistance and Retaliation

Though French civilians generally cooperated with the Germans, most resented their presence and the sight of the Nazi flag flying from public buildings. The French people called German soldiers *"verdigris,"* which means greenish-gray, the color of their uniforms. German soldiers were also called "Fritz" and "Boche"—derogatory slang terms.

In France as in other occupied countries, resistance groups tried to kill as many Germans as possible. Officers were a prime target. The Germans retaliated by executing French civilians and prisoners. A notice posted in Paris by the German authorities read, "Henceforth, all French people arrested will be considered hostages. When a hostile act occurs, a number of hostages commensurate with the seriousness of the act will be shot."[32] For every German officer who was killed, fifty or even one hundred French people were shot or publicly hanged, as in the

## The Spirit of Resistance

Claire Chevrillon, a Frenchwoman who worked for the resistance in Paris during World War II, went into hiding to escape the Gestapo. In her autobiography, *Code Name Christiane Clouet: A Woman in the French Resistance*, she writes about the beginning of a spirit of resistance among the French.

"At first the French people's hostility toward the Germans who had taken over our country showed itself in very modest ways. Certain writers and artists withdrew into silence. Posters were torn down or changed so they said the opposite of what was intended. . . . There were guffaws during the newsreels in the movie theaters. When a German soldier tried to start a conversation or wanted directions, he'd be met by blank stares."

As the occupation dragged on, the French engaged in other forms of resistance. Some were nonviolent, such as strikes and demonstrations. Other people gathered information and intelligence on German activity or sheltered people who were wanted by the Germans, such as Jews, people on the run from the Gestapo, or Allied airmen who had been shot down. In France, as in other occupied countries, people gathered clandestinely to listen to broadcasts of the BBC from London. There also existed in France a network for underground publishing and distribution of materials, ranging from banned novels to information pamphlets on the Nazis.

The Germans had to contend with more violent forms of resistance as well. One of the most common in France was sabotage on railways, which greatly slowed the movement of German troops and supplies. Small acts of sabotage hampered factory operations or damaged individual weapons and machines, but the Germans also faced full-scale armed guerrilla ambushes on troops and installations. The violence escalated as guerrilla attacks were met by German reprisals, and reprisals were met by further attacks.

town of Tulle, where the SS hanged ninety-nine men from the balconies of houses.

In February 1943, two *Luftwaffe* officers were shot and killed in an ambush behind the hotel in which they were quartered in Paris. In reprisal for their deaths, two thousand Jews were arrested and deported to a concentration camp. In the spring of 1944, an explosion halted a German troop train near Lille, France. No Germans were killed in the explosion, but the Germans retaliated by executing eighty-six civilians in a nearby village.

In the south of France in the Central Massif mountain range, groups of men known as Maquis secretly stored weapons and trained in anticipation of an Allied invasion. These guerrilla fighters ambushed individual trucks or convoys that carried food, clothing, fuel, weapons, or other supplies requisitioned from the French by the Nazis. German truck drivers were killed by the Maquis and the trucks commandeered. The Germans in France found themselves increasingly under attack by the Maquis. German troops were ambushed, Maquis hideouts were attacked, and eventually Germans and Maquis engaged in armed skirmishes and battles in the hills and streets of southern France. German retaliation was severe and often targeted civilians. In 1944, after defeating the local Maquis, the Germans executed nearly six hundred villagers in Oradour-sur-Glane, most of whom were women and children, by locking them inside a church and setting it ablaze.

*A German soldier flees Paris before Allied forces liberate the city.*

## Leaving Paris

After the Allies invaded the northern coast of France in June 1944, the Nazis were forced to leave the city of Paris in hasty retreat. Friedrich von Teuchert, a German soldier who had been stationed in Paris, recalls his last day in that historic city in August 1944:

> There were two green and white buses in front of the Royal Monceau [hotel]. We were to be packed up and out by three in the afternoon. Then came a surprise. I went to the mess. White linen and silver were on the table. The French staff offered us a farewell meal. There were six or seven servants, and not one behaved as if we were anything except habitual guests. They said they hoped we'd be back. That made a lasting impression.[33]

But for most German soldiers, leaving Paris was not a charming experience. A Frenchman in Paris on August 17, 1944—the day German forces withdrew from the city—describes what he calls

> the great flight of the Fritzes. . . . On every thoroughfare, scores, hundreds, of trucks, loaded cars, mounted artillery, ambulances full of wounded on stretchers, were in file or overtaking and crisscrossing one another. . . . In the rue Lafayette a flash of monocled generals sped past like shining torpedoes, accompanied by elegantly dressed blondes who seemed more on their way to some fashionable beach. Near the Galeries Lafayette, in front of his broken-down truck, a bespectacled soldier was trying fruitlessly to be towed by either French or Germans: at each refusal he smiled without losing his temper or his confidence. On his belt were long-handled grenades. On the terraces of the cafés along the boulevards and the avenue de l'Opéra, men from every branch of the forces continued drinking their beer. . . . At half past eight in the evening, trucks left, taking back to the Rhine the German personnel from the Trianon Hotel in the rue Vaugirard. . . . And suddenly, after the departure of the last truck, SS sentries on duty, automatic weapons at the ready, moved out toward the spectators, who panicked and scattered in all directions.[34]

## Return to Battle

In France and in the other occupied countries, as the tide of the war turned against Germany, instead of poorly armed resistance fighters the Nazi armies of occupation were forced to face the combined military might of the United States, Great Britain, and the Soviet Union. Instead of being the triumphant masters of the blitzkrieg, they were forced to fight battles of defense and retreat.

# The Eastern Front

Before dawn on June 22, 1941, just over 3 million German soldiers invaded the Soviet Union, beginning the biggest conflict in history fought along a single front. On any given day from June 1941 to May 1945, an average of 9 million troops were deployed by Germany and the Soviet Union on the eastern front. German soldiers pushed twelve hundred miles from Poland to Moscow in a little over two months, and then for the next three and a half years fought through retreats, new offensives, sieges, and further retreats, finally being pushed back fifteen hundred miles to Berlin. Soviet losses were staggering: Between 20 and 27 million soldiers and civilians were killed. Germany lost 3 million soldiers, and in the final stage of the war, when the Soviets forced the battle onto German soil, 2.5 million German civilians were killed.

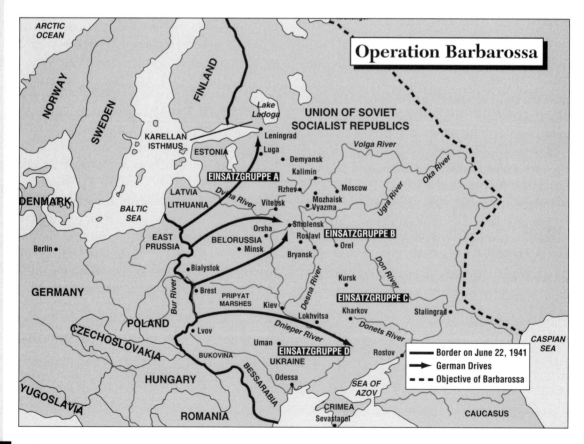

*A German gun crew celebrates the destruction of a Soviet tank during summer fighting in Russia in 1941.*

For German soldiers, going to war in the Soviet Union was a miserable experience. Few of them were used to living outdoors, but they had to adjust quickly to the rigors of cold and heat, snow, rain, mud, and dust. Life was full of discomfort and fear. Part of the fear was about the weather, especially the onset of winter. But they were also afraid of battle, both with the Red Army and with partisan groups. Even when German units were behind the front lines, they were not safe from attack. The rapid advance of the German forces during the invasion left many Russian soldiers stranded behind the lines. Often these professional soldiers banded together with civilians to fight the Germans using guerrilla tactics. The Germans made the situation more difficult for themselves by killing POWs, Jews, Communists, and other civilians. These actions made it clear to the Russians that they had nothing to lose by armed resistance: They were likely to be killed and preferred to die defending their homes and families. Thus, German soldiers were constantly under threat of attack.

The killing of POWs and civilians had been ordered by the Nazi regime. The orders, which violated the Hague and Geneva Conventions, were issued by the Wehrmacht High Command at Hitler's insistence. Some German soldiers tried to ignore the orders, but thousands participated in the slaughter of POWs and civilians.

## Early Success

As they had done in Poland and France, the German armed forces advanced rapidly in their invasion of the Soviet Union. Their major goal of the campaign, the capture of Moscow, seemed within reach a few short weeks after the offensive began. Hitler was so confident of victory that he diverted resources to other military goals, especially the defense of his territorial gains in western Europe. But the message from the front lines in the Soviet Union was not so clear.

The Soviet Union was the largest country in the world, but it was sparsely populated. Villages were as much as fifty miles apart. The

*Soviet soldiers surrender to a German Panzer crew in the Crimea in 1942.*

railway system was barely adequate to transport farm products and livestock. Even when resistance from the Soviet Red Army was light, the Germans had to keep their supply lines open and flowing—they could not always rely on capturing fuel and food in the Soviet Union. According to Siegfried Knappe, travel was grueling. The roads were often deeply rutted but also had areas of loose sand that offered poor traction. Marching troops and horse-drawn wagons raised thick clouds of dust, which coated everything and made breathing difficult. The sand and dust were so deep that walking required great effort and exhausted both men and horses.

Wehrmacht soldier Claus Hansmann wrote in his diary that during the march across the vast territory of the Soviet Union he and his fellow soldiers were

trudging along on tired legs . . . through the painfully seductive fragrance of the early summer steppe. The war must lose itself in the sweetness around here, but the weight of the equipment . . . violently forces us back into the present. The painful feet, the exhausted muscles speak the words of our obligation. . . . Each step is made agonizing by the heat and sweat. A fight against thirst, a fight against fatigue as well, finding the strength against the sun, weariness, and despair.[35]

## Noise and Lead

The Red Army did not always run away, though. Sometimes it stood and fought, and sometimes it attacked when least expected. The battles that ensued were unlike anything even seasoned German soldiers had known: tank attacks, devastating artillery barrages, and vast numbers of Soviet troops throwing themselves at the German lines. Knappe describes these battles in his memoir:

The sound of combat . . . was a virtual hurricane of noise, but it did not pass by as a hurricane does; it remained as long as the fighting went on. The roar of combat was the combined sounds of heavy artillery, light artillery, mortars, machine guns, hand grenades, rifles—every weapon used on the battlefield. The roar of combat alone was enough to shatter a soldier's will. But combat was a great deal more than just noise. It was a whirlwind of iron and lead that howled about the soldier, slicing through anything it hit. Even inside the roar of battle, strangely, the soldier could detect the whistle of bullets and the hum of slivers of shrapnel, perceiving everything separately—a shell burst here, the rattle of machine-gun fire over there, an enemy soldier hiding behind cover in another place.[36]

Guy Sajer once found himself in the middle of an artillery barrage that nearly buried him alive. He and his fellow soldiers watched the barrage begin, shells whistling toward them:

Then, with a cry of despair and a prayer for mercy, we dived to the bottom of our hole, trembling as the earth shook and

## The *Nebelwerfer*

During the invasion of Russia in 1941, the Germans introduced a new weapon that incited great fear in enemy troops: the *Nebelwerfer* (literally, smoke projector), a mobile rocket launcher. The development of the *Nebelwerfer* began in 1929. As military historian James Lucas explains in his book *War on the Eastern Front*, the Germans'

"interest in this type of propulsion went back to the Treaty of Versailles. Under its terms Germany was forbidden to have . . . tanks, aircraft, heavy artillery and the means to wage chemical warfare, but there were no clauses which specifically forbade the use of artificial smoke or the development of rockets. Consequently, in 1929, the High Command and the Reichswehr's Weapons Department used this loophole to seek an alternative to the heavy artillery which was forbidden."

Rockets had not been used extensively in battle before because they were inaccurate. Fins helped stabilize their flight, but they were often blown off course either by wind or by the uneven combustion of the rocket fuel. German engineer Walter Dornberger developed a solution to the problem. Instead of fins, Dornberger used small tubes placed at an angle in the exhaust outlet of the rocket to make it spin rapidly. This is the same principle that makes the flight of a football thrown with a spiral spin more stable and accurate. While still not as good as artillery, Dornberger's innovation improved accuracy enough to make rockets an effective weapon both with smoke shells (to disguise troop movements) and with high explosives. In addition, the rockets made a loud shrieking noise that evoked panic in enemy troops, who could hear the missile coming without knowing which way to run.

the intensity of our fear grew. The shocks, whose center seemed closer each time, were of an extraordinary violence. Torrents of snow and frozen earth poured down on us. A white flash, accompanied by an extraordinary displacement of air, and an intensity of noise which deafened us, lifted the edge of the trench. . . . We were thrown in a heap against the far wall of the hole. . . . Then, with a roar, the earth poured in and covered us. . . .

I was seized by a rush of terror so powerful that I felt my mind was cracking. Trapped by the weight of earth, I began to howl like a madman . . . and my whole body was gripped by a heavy and astonishingly inert substance which only held me more tightly the harder I struggled. Under my thigh I felt a leg kicking. . . . Something else was rubbing against my shoulder. . . . I pulled my head free of the dirt and of my helmet. . . . [T]wo feet from my face a horrible mask pouring blood was howling like a demon. . . .

My throat burst with screams of rage and despair. No nightmare could possibly reach

such a pitch of horror. At that moment, I suddenly understood the meaning of all the cries and shrieks I had heard on every battlefield.[37]

## The First Cold Weather

Perhaps the Soviet Union's most potent weapon was winter, when blizzards howled across the plains and temperatures dropped to thirty degrees below zero. The Red Army faced these conditions every year, had the proper clothing and equipment, and had developed survival skills for coping with the cold. The Germans, on the other hand, lacked all of these, and they knew that for the invasion to be successful, they would have to defeat the Soviets before winter set in. They failed.

Even in late fall, conditions became difficult for the German troops. Siegfried Knappe recalls that

a hard freeze came on November 7 [1941], which proved both an advantage and a disadvantage. We could move again [because the mud had frozen], but now

*Captured Nazis in Moscow in December 1941 show the effects of the Russian winter.*

# The Loss of a Comrade

When Siegfried Knappe was wounded in a Soviet tank attack, his fellow officer Karl Schumann was wounded as well. Knappe and Schumann were dragged from the battlefield on sleds and then taken by truck to a hospital. During the long, cold, painful ride, Knappe folded his blanket into a pillow to keep Schumann's head from bouncing on the truck bed. In his memoir *Soldat*, Knappe writes that he was treated and then sent back to Poland to recover, but Schumann was not so fortunate.

"Schumann was too seriously wounded to travel, so they kept him at the hospital in Vyazma, where he later died. I had known him since France, so we had been together over a year—a long time in combat. We were not close friends, but he had been a good comrade and fellow soldier. . . . At

thirty-one, he was old for his rank, because he had been promoted through the ranks instead of attending a military academy, a practice that had begun with the start of the war in 1939. Unfortunately, such people were looked down upon by many officers. Many of them were as good or even better than the rest of us as officers, because they had more practical experience, but they were not as educated or as sophisticated. There was even a bad joke about them. They were called 'vomags,' a term composed of the first letters of the expression 'folk officer with a laborer's face.' It was a very degrading expression. Schumann had felt the insult keenly, but he had borne it manfully and showed no resentment or bitterness. He had been a good soldier and a good officer—and now he had given all he had for folk and Fatherland."

we were freezing because we still did not have winter clothing. We had the same field uniforms we had worn during the summer, plus a light overcoat. It seemed inexplicable that they could not get winter clothing to us. . . . We tried to spend the nights in villages so we could get out of the weather. In November this far north, we had only seven hours of daylight. We would start well before daylight and keep going long after dark because of the short hours of daylight. As long as we marched, of course, our physical movement kept us from freezing.[38]

Knappe recounts that as the weather got colder, the troops began hearing a long list of excuses for not receiving their winter uniforms, and they became more and more desperate for some relief from the cold:

Some of our soldiers took felt boots from dead Russian soldiers, but we did not dare risk wearing their heavier quilted jackets for fear of being shot for a Russian. Fortunately, we could pull the flaps of our field caps down to keep our ears from freezing. The men wrapped their blankets about themselves, over their overcoats and caps, and cursed those responsible for not providing us with winter clothing.[39]

## The Advance Stalls

The colder the weather, the slower the German advance. Finally, German troops were literally frozen in their tracks. One German lieutenant commented on the weather that halted his unit in December 1941: "Icy snowstorms swept over the land and obstructed our vision. . . . The ground was so slick that the horses had difficulty even standing up. Because of the cold our machine guns wouldn't work at all."[40] And as Knappe recalls:

As we approached the outermost suburbs of Moscow a paralyzing blast of cold hit us, and the temperature dropped far below zero and stayed there. Our trucks and vehicles would not start, and our horses started to die from the cold in large numbers. . . . The Russians knew how to cope with this weather, but we did not; their vehicles were built and conditioned for this kind of weather, but ours were not. We all now numbly wrapped ourselves in our blankets. Everyone felt brutalized and defeated by the cold. . . . Frostbite was taking a very heavy toll now as more and more men were sent back to the field hospitals with frozen fingers and toes.[41]

## Winter

During the winter of 1941–1942, the Germans were pushed back but not out of the Soviet Union. The Germans spent the next three winters fighting, freezing, and dying in the Soviet Union before they were finally defeated in the spring of 1945. Though the war on the eastern front was long and complex, the basic pattern that developed was that the Germans would mount new offensives in the late spring and summer of each year, often achieving some victories, only to lose ground each winter. The Wehrmacht got better at fighting in the cold, but the problems of waging war with a thousand-mile-long supply line were simply insurmountable. Germany's defeats often resulted from the obvious, day-to-day obstacles that no amount of ideological commitment could overcome.

For example, Guy Sajer describes the difficulties involved in getting his motorized unit going in the morning:

We had to roll out barrels of gasoline and alcohol to fill the gas tanks and radiators, crank up the engines [by hand]—an exhausting labor—and shovel out cubic yards of snow, almost entirely without light. When the fifteen trucks were ready, we set out . . . following the bumpy, snow-covered track. . . . One of the trucks skidded on the icy ground, and it took a good half hour to pull it from the ditch. We hooked it to another truck, which could only skate along the ice. In the end, almost the entire company was involved in the struggle, and we literally carried the damn machine back onto the road.[42]

When snowstorms struck, they were like nothing the Germans had known at home, and even everyday tasks became life-threatening; becoming lost in winter meant almost certain death. German soldier Claus Hansmann describes struggling through a blizzard to find the house where he was billeted:

You're propelled like a withered leaf. . . . You forge on, and step by step you press on into the icy wall of snow that threatens you. Your head sunk low, a bit sideways with open mouth, snatching at breath, you carefully set one foot in front of the other. First you take a strong step, then tense your muscles powerfully, and you notice that slowly your body moves forward. So you fight against the elements, a small, tiny man all alone. . . . You go on, always forward. Forward? You must have reached the house at last? You carefully raise your face somewhat against the storm and squint for a few seconds into the white force. . . . But everything is a torrent, everything is snow in raging movement. You are alone.[43]

In the very coldest weather, even the Red Army usually refrained from attacking, so the main concern of the Germans was finding food and shelter and waiting out the storms. But they still had to go out on patrol—looking for partisans and early signs of Red Army attacks—see to their animals, and perform other tasks. According to Wehrmacht soldier Harry Mielert, blizzards could leave a unit lost and stranded without warning:

[I]n a few minutes the most well-trodden paths and trails are obliterated, whole villages are totally snow-covered, you can't orient yourself on anything, . . . no one can find their way. . . . We are in a terrible situation. Nothing more is to be seen of our trenches. . . . You can only tell where the bunkers are by sighting a straw flag on a pole stuck above them. Every path, every trail is gone within a few minutes.[44]

## Overwhelming Force

Though in many ways the Germans were better trained and equipped than the Russians, in the end it was Russia's massive number of soldiers and immense industrial capacity that spelled defeat for the Germans. In 1942, for instance, the Soviets produced 24,000 armored vehicles and 21,700 aircraft versus Germany's 4,800 vehicles and 14,700 planes.

## Hunger

On the eastern front in 1944 and 1945, as the Germans were in retreat and their supply systems were breaking down, the search for food was the German soldier's biggest concern. According to Guy Sajer in his memoir *Forgotten Soldier*, "We became hunters and trappers and nest robbers, and experimented with wild plants whose leaves looked like salad greens. After a long chase, we were sometimes able to catch an abandoned horse. But eight hundred men require substantial quantities of food." Sajer wrote that in his unit, soldiers were killed on the suspicion that they might be hiding food, but generally such suspicions proved untrue.

Hans Woltersdorf was wounded in battle and had one leg partially amputated. He and another soldier named Rase lived in a railway car while they were waiting to be evacuated. He is quoted in Stephen Fritz's book *Frontsoldaten*.

"There was simply nothing at all to eat. . . . Rase still had all his limbs and was constantly out and about. . . . He brought leaves, grasses, and herbs and . . . knew what could be done with them. . . . Rase sized up my good leg and drew to my attention what a waste it was that I had not brought along the sawn-off leg as a reserve supply. . . . There would certainly have been a usable joint of some kilos left above the knee. . . . And so the only bit of hope remaining for me and Rase was that when the follow-up amputation was done on my leg, some extra kilos of flesh could be cut off and saved for consumption."

Fritz speculates that some cannibalism probably occurred among German soldiers during the Battle of Stalingrad (September 1942–February 1943) and in the last days of the war, when all the usual systems for keeping track of wounded men had broken down and many were left unattended.

For most of the war, the Soviets had twice as many men at the front as the Germans. On June 1, 1944, the Soviets had 476 divisions, 37 tank and mechanized corps, 93 artillery divisions, and 14,787 combat aircraft. The German strength on the eastern front was a small fraction of that, not to mention that five days later Germany would face the largest sea and air invasion in history on the beaches of northern France.

In Russia the Germans had to face a new kind of battle. At times the Soviets threw huge masses of troops into battle even when there was no hope of winning. Sajer reports that on one occasion, the Soviets sent a human wave of soldiers into a minefield in an attempt to clear a path: "The minefield exploded under the howling mob, and we sent out a curtain of yellow and white fire to obliterate anyone who had survived. The fragmented cadavers froze very quickly, sparing us the stench which would otherwise have polluted the air over a vast area."[45] Virtually the same thing happened to Knappe's unit: Five hundred infantry soldiers attacked his artillery company across an open field.

> We could see them moving about three kilometers away. [We] opened fire on them, but they kept coming. It was just suicide, because they were out in the open and they had no tanks or artillery or protection of any kind. They got as close as two hundred meters before they were completely decimated. . . . Hundreds of dead and wounded lay in the reddened snow, horribly mangled and spattered with blood, their eyes growing dim as their lives ran out.[46]

Though these Soviet attacks failed, others succeeded. And even when the Soviet human wave tactics failed, they made the Germans fear that the Soviets had a virtually unlimited number of soldiers and that there was simply no way to defeat such massive troop concentrations.

## A New Reason to Fight

As the war on the eastern front dragged on, as German soldiers became hungrier, more ragged, more exhausted and despondent, their original idealism—their zeal to defend Germany and make it safe from communism and "subhuman" Slavic hordes—faded and even died. As Guy Sajer explains:

> Faced with the Russian hurricane, we ran whenever we could. . . . We no longer

*The stress of unrelenting continuous combat in Russia shows on the faces of these veterans of the Russian front.*

fought for Hitler, or for National Socialism, or for the Third Reich—or even for our fiancées or mothers or families trapped in bomb-ravaged towns. We fought from simple fear. . . . We fought for reasons which are perhaps shameful, but are, in the end, stronger than any doctrine. We fought for ourselves, so that we wouldn't die in holes filled with mud and snow; we fought like rats, which do not hesitate to spring with all their teeth bared when they are cornered.[47]

## Being Wounded

For German soldiers, being wounded was sometimes seen as a blessing—if it resulted in being sent well behind the lines to recover. But even that meant danger and anxiety. Nowhere in the Soviet Union were German soldiers completely safe, and medical evacuation trucks and trains could be attacked by the Red Army or partisan groups at any time. The ability of the Wehrmacht medical corps to care for the wounded was stretched to the breaking point, and many German soldiers died simply because there was no one to take care of them or, when medics were available, a lack of supplies.

Shortly after his unit reached the outskirts of Moscow, Knappe was wounded in the arm and head during an attack by Soviet tanks. Though neither wound was life-threatening, he apparently sustained a concussion and lost his sense of balance. It was early December 1941, and the temperature was near zero. Nevertheless, he and others wounded in the attack were taken in the back of an open truck over bumpy roads to a field hospital in Vyazma, seventy-five miles behind the lines. There he was put on a train for Warsaw, Poland, but he had not been deloused—lice got under his bandages where he could not get to them, causing excruciating itching.

Claus Hansmann describes regaining consciousness after he was wounded and then being transported to a hospital on a stretcher:

Your head rolls weakly to the side, and your mouth opens, your tongue seeking cool drops. . . .

Someone carries you on a stretcher. . . . Slowly distant impressions sink into your consciousness: the crunching of footsteps, voices, the smells of soldier's [sic] coats. . . . But what are these men saying? This damned fog! If you could only understand these sounds. . . . That must be Russian they are speaking above you! . . . You are so cold and clammy, can just raise your head over the edge of the stretcher, then your whole stomach seems to spring up. . . .

You are lifted up, get tablets and cool water that you eagerly slurp. . . . Unrest all through the night hours, then it is morning. Through the buzzing rumors of many men rings clear: "Comrades! The ambulance column can't make it through, . . . they are waiting for us twenty-five kilometers from here. The time is short, we must withdraw. . . ."

Then quite a few shots reverberate! Is that Ivan [the Soviets] already? Anxiety, panic bursts into the open. Everyone's petrified. . . .

Something shoots like an electric current through the group! Ahead under a tree a waving form. . . . a soldier. Already from a distance he shouts: "Just five kilometers, Comrades!" . . . The steps become more confident. . . . Slowly the suffering column leaves the darkness of the forest. . . . Finally . . . the muffled echo of an entrance door. . . . Now it's your turn, again you're carried, along quiet, long corridors full of hospital air. Through a door a bright room, a voice: it is a woman! Everything is all right.[48]

## Germans and Russians

The Slavic and Asiatic peoples of the Soviet Union were considered subhuman by the Nazis, and the Soviet countryside was barren, unfamiliar, harsh, and dangerous for German soldiers. According to historian Stephen Fritz, these factors "converged to produce a unique kind of horror [and] a mind-set of hatred, so that the [German soldier] came to see himself as fighting to protect the German community from 'Asiatic-Jewish' influences out to destroy the Reich." Fritz believes that the average German soldier in the Soviet Union felt himself "free to engage in virtually any criminal behavior, be it plunder, rape, or murder, as long as it was directed against so-called racial enemies of the German Volk; he was not only rarely punished but often praised for his racial and ideological consciousness."[49]

Even in the early days of the campaign against the Soviet Union it was obvious to Ger-

German troops question an old Russian woman who lives in a shell hole. Soviet citizens feared the Nazi invaders would kill them.

man soldiers that the number of prisoners they were taking could not be properly taken care of. Siegfried Knappe reports that he knew about the Commissar Order (a directive to German commanders to kill all Communist Party officials accompanying the Soviet army) but claims he did not know that Communist officials would be killed, and then says that they were killed by the Nazi Party (meaning the SS), not the Wehrmacht. In fact, by the time of the invasion of the Soviet Union, the SS was no longer merely a Nazi Party organization but an agency of the government, and the Wehrmacht was involved in atrocities against Soviet civilians and POWs from the beginning of the campaign. What Knappe actually knew at the time is impossible to determine, but according to scholars such as Omer Bartov, the attempt to put the blame on the Nazis rather than the Wehrmacht is typical of many German veterans.

The Red Army committed atrocities as well, often killing German soldiers after they had surrendered. Then there was a further escalation in brutality: The system of military justice in the German armed forces, especially as it treated cases of desertion and disobedience, became much more harsh than in any other modern army. As many as fifteen thousand German soldiers were executed by their own army during the war, compared with forty British and one hundred French soldiers. In other words, conditions on the eastern front were harsh first because the Germans saw the war as racial, one of annihilation and subjugation of an entire people, and the Soviets responded in kind, making it that much more likely that German soldiers would try to avoid battle entirely. Then in order to keep their soldiers in the fight, the Germans made death the punishment for behavior that even hinted at desertion. Their purpose was to make German soldiers fear their own commanders more than they feared the enemy.

## Army of Retribution

The German soldier's greatest fear—that the Soviets would defeat them, invade Germany, and wreak revenge on the German people—was realized in the final days of the war. The Red Army was turned loose for an orgy of destruction, rape, and murder that was exceeded only by the violence and cruelty that the Germans had inflicted on the Soviet Union earlier in the war. Thousands of German soldiers deserted and went west to surrender to the British and American armies, but many of them were later turned over to the Soviets. They were imprisoned in the Soviet Union for up to ten years, and a large percentage of them never saw Germany again, dying in captivity in the country they had fought so hard to destroy.

# The Afrika Korps: "To the Last Bullet"

"*Heia Safari!*"—Swahili for "Let's go get 'em!"—was the battle cry of the Afrika Korps, the German troops sent to bolster the Italians, their partners in the Axis alliance, who controlled much of North Africa. In early 1941, the Italians were in retreat from a British offensive, and Hitler feared that the Allies would soon win a strategic advantage. Hitler sent one of his most trusted commanders, Major General (later Field Marshal) Erwin Rommel and the 5th Light and 15th Panzer Divisions to rescue the Italians from certain defeat. Rommel and the Afrika Korps soon became a legendary force, waging war in the deserts of Libya, Egypt, and Tunisia against Allied forces for the next two years.

## Newcomers to the Desert

In February 1941, when the first two divisions of the Afrika Korps arrived in the port city of Tripoli in western Libya, none of its units had trained to fight a desert campaign. As Ronald Lewin writes in *The Life and Death of the Afrika Korps*, "No attention had been given to research and development of appropriate equipment. No war games or even more modest exercises had examined tactical problems. The orientation, the training and the armament of the force that finally disembarked at Tripoli were entirely those of a formation designed for European conditions."[50] Rommel, who led this force into North Africa, had never even set foot in the desert.

Despite their lack of proper training and equipment, the men of the Afrika Korps adapted to fighting in unfamiliar terrain and developed a strong sense of identity. The credit for their successes in the desert goes largely to Rommel, known worldwide as the Desert Fox for his ability to outwit his opponents in battle. As one biographer of Rommel puts it,

*The leader of Germany's Afrika Korps, Field Marshal Erwin Rommel.*

# The Rommel Phenomenon

The considerable impression Rommel made upon his enemies prompted General Auchinleck, commander of Britain's Middle Eastern forces in North Africa, to write a warning about the Rommel phenomenon. The following order, reprinted in Desmond Young's *Rommel: The Desert Fox*, was issued to all British commanders and chiefs of staff in North Africa:

"There exists a real danger that . . . Rommel is becoming a kind of magician or bogeyman to our troops, who are talking far too much about him. He is by no means a su-perman, although he is undoubtedly very energetic and able. Even if he were a superman, it would still be highly undesirable that our men should credit him with supernatural powers.

I wish you to dispel by all possible means the idea that Rommel represents something more than an ordinary German general. The important thing now is to see that we do not always talk of Rommel when we mean the enemy in Libya. We must refer to 'the Germans' or 'the Axis powers' or 'the enemy' and not always keep harping on Rommel."

---

Rommel *was* the Afrika Korps, to his own men as well as to the enemy. It was he who made them bold, self-confident and even arrogant in battle. It was he who taught them to pull the last ounce out of themselves and never to admit that they were beaten. It was because they were the Afrika Korps that, even when they were taken prisoner, they marched down to the docks at Suez with their heads high, still whistling "We march against England to-day."[51]

## Conditions in the Desert

Despite their devotion to their commander, German soldiers in North Africa found the desert an inhospitable place. Temperatures could fluctuate by as much as sixty degrees within a single day. Even in the summer, the nights were cold and men had to wear their tunics and scarves for warmth well after sunrise. Daytime heat was often compounded by hot winds, which could blow at up to ninety miles per hour and raise temperatures by as much as thirty-five degrees in a couple of hours. The *ghibli*—the Arabic word for the wind—could last up to three days and caused blinding sandstorms that left the men gasping for air.

The sand was a constant menace to the Afrika Korps. Troop movements and battles were often hampered by decreased visibility in sandstorms. The blowing sand inflamed their eyes, filled their nostrils, and gritted between their teeth. Troops wore dust goggles and masks—sometimes fashioned makeshift out of a handkerchief or scarf—for protection against sandstorms. Sand buried equipment, covered food, and blew into vehicles and tents. Fine sand clogged their rifles and the air filters on vehicles. Sand also got into wounds, which frequently became infected; gauze dressings were necessary to protect even the smallest sores.

Scorpions, vipers, and flies were another constant menace in the desert. Soldiers were attacked by swarms of flies, and wounds were also a prime target for the pests. Parasites, malnutrition, and poor hygiene made soldiers in the desert susceptible to outbreaks of dysentery,

*In Africa, water was often more precious than bullets. The German Afrika Korps required fifteen hundred tons of water a day.*

underlying layer of limestone—a time-consuming and difficult process. Water was so precious and so hard to come by in the desert that not a drop was wasted; dirty water was reused in vehicle radiators by filtering it through a cloth.

Soldiers dug slit trenches for protection from shelling, sandstorms, and cold nights. Because the limestone was so hard, the trenches were shallow and narrow—usually only big enough for one or two men. Because of the many advances and retreats during the desert campaign, German soldiers often reused their own or enemy slit trenches. Dried-up waterways, called *wadis*, were also used for cover.

## Leisure Time

In the desert, there was not much to do during leisure time besides lounge in the sun or swat flies. If the men happened to be stationed near the coast they were able to swim in the Mediterranean. Farther inland, gazelle hunting was a popular sport.

The Germans also listened to the radio, tuning in every evening to the German-run Radio Belgrade to hear their favorite song, "Lili Marlene." Sung in German by Lale Anderson, this song became the unofficial anthem of the Afrika Korps. They also listened to enemy broadcasts. Lieutenant Heinz Werner Schmidt, Rommel's aide, explains in his memoirs:

> Although it was against orders, we listened every night to the news and to music broadcast from Cairo. The British had a fairly objective propaganda station there. We learned from [British] Eighth Army prisoners that they too listened to the "enemy," particularly to hear *Lili Marlene* played from Belgrade or Athens. The sentimental tune reminded us on

scurvy, malaria, and other diseases. Jaundice, a yellowing of the skin usually caused by liver disease, was a particularly common problem; Rommel had liver problems resulting in jaundice throughout most of the African campaign.

The vastness of the desert made it difficult to transport supplies and reinforcements to the front lines. Everything had to be brought in by truck over long distances, and German convoys were vulnerable to British air attacks along the way. Some supply lines ran through minefields. To circumvent these problems, German Stuka dive-bombers or HE 111 bombers sometimes dropped supplies while on reconnaissance flights.

The German army in North Africa required fifteen hundred tons of water a day. They had to drill deep for water, through an both sides that there were other things than aerial bombs and Desert warfare.[52]

Both Paris and Rome were popular destinations for German soldiers on leave from Africa. With no blackout and few military vehicles, Rome seemed virtually unaffected by the war. Hans Luck writes of his leave in Rome, "In my faded tropical uniform, I felt out of place."[53] Indeed, soldiers were often surprised by the contrast between the front lines in the desert and the streets of Rome. Schmidt writes of his leave in Rome:

Within days of being in a bloody and historic action, I found myself walking the peaceful streets of the Eternal City, with elegant women and debonair men frequenting restaurants where life was suave and luxurious.

How sensible and sensuous at the same time the joy of a fawning barber—to have a haircut, a shampoo, a shave, a face massage, and a manicure from a glittering blonde! I ate ice-cream in a café and looked at the beautiful women who passed.[54]

Men also went home on leave to visit families and girlfriends. A few soldiers spent their time on leave sitting in on university lectures, catching up on studies missed while at the front.

## Rations

The basic rations for German soldiers in the desert were black bread and canned meat such as sardines and sausage. Schmidt writes in his memoirs, "Fruit and vegetables are unknown to the soldier. They miss their potatoes especially. The usual rations consist of sardines in oil, bulky tinned-meat sausages (*Bierwurst*), and 'Alter Mann.'"[55] *Alter Mann*, German for "old man," was what the Afrika Korps called the Italian tins of tough beef.

## New Year's Eve 1941

During the first holiday season of the desert campaign, the Afrika Korps were ordered to conserve their ammunition, which had been spent in recent fighting. Lieutenant Heinz Werner Schmidt and his troops on the front line felt that some sort of celebration was in order for New Year's Eve, however, so they made plans in secret. Schmidt describes their celebration in his memoirs, *With Rommel in the Desert*:

"On the stroke of midnight on New Year's Eve every position as far as the eye could see contributed its share to a first-class exhibition of fireworks. Light 'flak' and machine-guns fired tracers. Every available Very pistol pumped up red, green, and white flares. Hand-grenades, which we had so far used but little, went off with a most satisfactory bang. Even some big guns belched forth into the heavens, or into the distant Desert. The din was terrific, and the desolate countryside was lit up for miles. The display lasted for precisely three minutes and then darkness and silence descended on the Desert once more.

We were as pleased as truant schoolboys when, from the dark distance where we knew the screen of British tanks lay, a counter-display of yellow Very flares also went up to greet the New Year.

Not a word of reproof came down the line from Rommel or his generals."

# Uniforms and Equipment

The tropical uniforms issued to the Afrika Korps were ill suited for the desert. They were khaki-colored, made of a tightly woven fabric, and cut to fit close to the body, thus offering poor air circulation. Troops were also issued high lace-up boots and pith helmets. Tank crewmen wore black Panzer Group uniforms. Italian uniforms were looser fitting and made of lighter material; German soldiers often traded with the Italians for more suitable and comfortable shirts and trousers. Many soldiers of the Afrika Korps wore shorts with their tunics to cope with the heat. In the desert, all uniforms quickly became faded and covered with dust.

All soldiers were issued a compass, which Luck refers to as "the most important instrument, carried by everyone"[56] because it was so easy to become lost in the desert. Unfortunately, electrical disturbances from sandstorms frequently threw off compass readings, sometimes with disastrous results as soldiers advanced unawares into enemy territory or minefields.

Another piece of equipment essential in the desert was the water can. These sturdy metal receptacles held four and a half gallons of water and were carried in trucks and armored personnel carriers and strapped to the outside of tanks.

## Tanks and Armaments

The open expanse of the desert was ideal tank country. Early in the campaign the Afrika Korps used the dust to its advantage to conceal from the British the fact that they had fewer tanks. Rommel staged a parade in Tripoli using dummy tanks made of cardboard, wood, and canvas and mounted on automobile chassis. He ordered the Panzers to head the formations, while the dummy tanks followed in the dust in the rear. This parade of the so-called Cardboard Division was quite successful in mis-

*Two of a German soldier's best friends: the Panzerkampfwagen IV (left) and the 88 mm antiaircraft/antitank gun (right).*

leading the British about the might of the Afrika Korps.

Although fewer in number, the German Panzer IIIs and Panzer IVs were lighter, faster, and better armed than the British Matildas. In addition, the Afrika Korps used 88-mm antiaircraft guns against British tanks—something that had never before been done—with great success. Firing twenty-two-pound shells, these antiaircraft guns could tear large holes in Matildas at a distance of up to a mile. The German Panzers were unmatched and seemed unstoppable—until the arrival in May 1942 of American-built M3 Grant tanks, and later that same year the M4 Sherman tank. The virtually impenetrable Sherman tanks shook the morale of the Afrika Korps and were a key factor in their eventual defeat.

## The Afrika Korps in Action

The Afrika Korps won many swift victories upon their arrival in the desert, but they failed to take the strategically important Libyan port city of Tobruk, which was held by two Australian brigades. Rommel knew that as he drove east into Egypt, these Australian troops would be left behind his advancing Panzers and could attack his supply lines. Schmidt writes about coming under enemy fire and using a tank for cover during the first attempt to take Tobruk:

> Before we realized what was happening we found ourselves in a real hubbub. Shell-bursts, anti-tank missiles whizzing by, and the rat-tat-tat of machine-guns left us in no doubt that we had made a sudden appearance under the noses of the enemy. With lightning speed we leapt from the car and dived for protection behind the Panzer. We clutched at it, haul-

*A column of German armor races across the desert of North Africa.*

> ing our legs up to avoid the bursts of machine-gun bullets which were splashing knee-high against the caterpillars of the tank. . . . The driver of the tank started to turn sharply and was on the point of exposing our behinds to the enemy when a rear-track snapped.

> In these circumstances there was only one course to adopt. On the heels of the driver, who had already left his turret and was taking flying leaps towards the side of the road, we plunged into a group of deep shell-holes.[57]

Taking the British-held fortress of Tobruk became an important cause to Rommel and the Afrika Korps. Finally, in June 1942, after

# German Prisoners of War

The book *For Führer and Fatherland*, by Roderick de Norman, describes the process Nazi soldiers underwent when taken prisoner. Like those taken captive in Tunis, German POWs were immediately disarmed and relieved of any documentation, maps, and other paperwork they carried. Prisoners were required to identify themselves by their name, rank, and unit. To break down any sense of prisoner cohesion, officers were immediately separated from the rest of the men and held in "barbed wire enclosures of a simple type, capable of holding 250 men."

The British and their allies used three methods for obtaining information from prisoners: direct questioning, concealed microphones, and "stool pigeons." De Norman stresses that these interrogations were "heavily regulated by the Geneva Convention. At no time were interrogators permitted to use physical violence on a prisoner and there are no incidents recorded in the archives to suggest that detailed interrogators ever did."

After interrogation, German POWs were classified based on their political nature. Each man was graded White, Grey, or Black, as De Norman explains:

"'Whites' were those judged to be 'anti-Nazi' and who might be persuaded to work actively for the Allies, either in the camps themselves or in such diverse tasks as broadcasting to Germany or those countries still occupied. The 'Greys' were those POWs who showed themselves not to have any particular political allegiance but were thought unlikely to work for the Allies. 'Blacks,' however, were those prisoners who showed true loyalty to Hitler and National Socialism during their screenings. These prisoners would have to be watched very carefully and on the whole, most were sent to Canada or America."

seven months and two previous failed attempts, Rommel's Afrika Korps launched a surprise attack from the southeast and managed to drive the British out of Tobruk in less than twenty-four hours. By this time the Germans had turned the numbers around—their tanks now outnumbered the British four to one. The Afrika Korps suffered 2,500 casualties in the battle of Tobruk. They captured 2,000 vehicles—including 30 British tanks—400 guns, 2,000 tons of fuel, 5,000 tons of provisions, and many tons of ammunition. According to historian Kenneth Macksey, it was "the greatest victory Rommel would ever win,"[58] and afterward he was promoted to field marshal. Morale in the Afrika Korps after Tobruk was at an all-time high.

## Wounded in Action

During the siege of Tobruk, pinned down by enemy fire, some German soldiers faced a moment of doubt when they believed death was imminent. Schmidt describes his feelings when he was wounded:

> Now I was certain that my fate was sealed. My mouth was dry, my lips parched. I thought of home. So this, then, was the end, in a miserable hole in the dirt in Africa. . . .
>
> Then I felt a severe slap on the rump, and simultaneously an avalanche of sand almost buried my head. I knew that I had been hit. But at once I felt strangely

at peace. What did death matter, after all?[59]

Schmidt survived his wound, but because he was in the midst of an ongoing battle, he had to wait for treatment and risked infection, as did many German soldiers. A severe shortage of supplies meant that some soldiers underwent surgery without anesthetic. Luck was wounded in the groin in 1942 and, after spending five days under morphine on the front lines during the siege of Tobruk, he was flown to Italy for treatment. He describes the grisly scene in his memoirs:

> It was then decided to perform a small operation and I was told that the limited anesthetics were needed for very severe cases. "Clench your teeth, please," I was instructed, short and sharp. While two sisters [nurses] held me tight, the doctor, who seemed to me like a butcher, began to cut away at my wound. I cried out like an animal and thought I would faint with pain.[60]

## The Afrika Korps in Retreat

The British commander in North Africa, Bernard Montgomery, on the defensive up to this point, decided to pound the Germans into surrender or retreat. He launched a massive artillery and infantry attack that began at El Alamein, Egypt, the farthest point of the German advance toward their ultimate goal of taking control of the Suez Canal. On the night of October 23, 1942, nine hundred guns fired a barrage into the German lines in an explosion that could be heard in Alexandria, sixty miles away. "Nearly a thousand guns flashed and roared simultaneously against us that night," writes Schmidt. "The earth from the Qattara Depression to the Mediterranean quaked. Far back from the front line, men were jarred to their teeth."[61]

The Germans were badly outnumbered: 104,000 German troops and 496 German tanks faced 195,000 British troops and 1,029 British tanks. The Germans were also outnumbered two to one in antitank guns and artillery. And, whereas the British Eighth Army was well supplied, the Afrika Korps was suffering from shortages of everything, receiving only a fifth of the supplies they requested.

When the British attack began, Rommel was in Austria undergoing treatment for his liver ailment. Only a few hours into the battle, General Georg Stumme, who had taken over in Rommel's absence, suffered a fatal heart attack. The Afrika Korps was without a leader until Rommel cut his treatment short and returned to Africa. His return had a great effect on the morale of the Afrika Korps, but it was not enough to turn the tide of the battle for El Alamein in their favor. Ronald Lewin writes that Rommel was preparing as orderly a retreat as he could manage when, on November 3, Hitler ordered him "to hold out to the last man and the last round."[62] Rommel wrestled with his conscience the rest of the day, finally deciding to obey Hitler's order as best he could. But by November 5, the British attack had advanced so far that Rommel saw retreat as the only option. With fuel and ammunition supplies virtually exhausted, the Afrika Korps withdrew to the west. Three days later, Rommel described to Hans Luck

> the terrible scenes that were taking place in the coastal road. Pursued by British tanks and covered inescapably by carpets of bombs, vehicles were left standing in flames, while the men tried to save themselves on foot. . . . [Rommel said,] "Through Hitler's crazy order to hold out,

we lost a vital day, which cost us losses that cannot be made good."[63]

In the retreat from El Alamein, thirty thousand German soldiers were captured by the British and spent the rest of the war in POW camps.

## Tunis: Regroup and Attack

The Afrika Korps was in full retreat along the coast road from El Alamein to Tunis, a distance of two thousand miles. This grim situation worsened on the morning of November 8 when a joint American and British force of over one hundred thousand landed at nine points in northwest Africa. After securing positions there, the Allies began moving east toward Tunis. It seemed that Rommel and his troops were finished, that even if they reached Tunis, they would be crushed by Montgomery's forces from the east and the newly arrived Allied army from the west. But the Germans made one more play for victory.

During Rommel's retreat, Hitler sent a new Panzer army to Tunis under the command of General Juergen von Arnim. Tunis was the most defensible spot for the Germans in North Africa. It was close to Axis bases in Sicily and so was relatively easy to supply. It was also protected by mountain ranges to the west and man-made fortifications to the east that the Germans quickly took advantage of. In fact, by February 1943 Arnim and Rommel were able to launch attacks against the Allies. The Germans had some success, but by early March Rommel

*A German soldier is stripped of his Iron Cross after surrendering to Allied forces in Tunisia.*

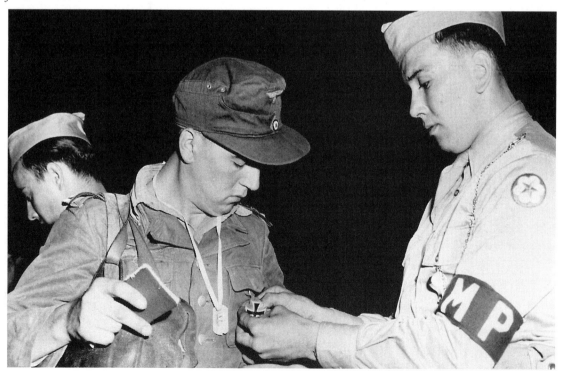

realized that the Allies' vast resources of men and weapons would soon overwhelm the Afrika Korps.

On March 6, Rommel lost fifty-two tanks in an engagement with Montgomery's forces. Three days later Rommel flew to Germany to try to persuade Hitler to abandon North Africa so that the Afrika Korps could live to fight other battles. Hitler refused and relieved Rommel of command, telling him to go on sick leave.

## The Last Days of the Afrika Korps

Rommel's departure left Arnim in command, but his ammunition and fuel were nearly depleted and his soldiers were subsisting on two slices of bread per day. As the German defenses collapsed, Hitler sent Arnim the following order: "The German people expect you to fight to the last bullet."[64] There was little Arnim could do, however. He kept his tanks moving until they ran out of fuel and then fired a final, futile salvo at the Allies.

On the eve of the surrender, the Afrika Korps transmitted its final radio signal to the German High Command. The message, whose closing salutation was perhaps a snub of Hitler, encapsulates the high morale of the Afrika Korps even in defeat: "Ammunition shot off. Arms and equipment destroyed. In accordance with orders received Afrika Korps has fought itself to the condition where it can fight no more. The German Afrika Korps must rise again. Heil Safari!"[65]

The end came with Arnim's surrender to the Allies on May 13, 1943. German losses at Tunis included 18,594 dead and 3,400 missing. More than 130,000 German soldiers lay down their arms and went into captivity, while 663 managed to escape. Those taken prisoner were sent to POW camps in Canada, Great Britain, and the United States to wait out the war.

# War Crimes

I n every war, some soldiers obey the rules and others break them. And in every war, there are differences between the rules of war and what armies order, encourage, or allow their soldiers to do. The 1907 Hague Convention and 1929 Geneva Convention set the rules applicable in World War II: Civilians were to be left alone as much as possible, and when an enemy soldier surrendered he was to be removed from battle, given medical attention, and adequately housed and fed. All the countries that participated in World War II violated the rules to some degree, but for the Nazis, killing POWs and civilians was central to their military objectives—to give Germany *Lebensraum* (living space) and safe borders, ending any threat from the "subhuman" Jews and Slavs. Thus, German soldiers were ordered to kill civilians and POWs, sometimes through explicit instructions, at other times through vaguely worded suggestions, but at all times with the understanding that atrocities would go unpunished and might even be rewarded.

## The German Army and the Jews

German soldiers were taught that Jews were subhuman. Adolf Hitler and other members of the Nazi military hierarchy blamed Jews for Germany's defeat in World War I, for the Great Depression, for the rise of communism in Russia, and for the rise of capitalism in the West. The Nazis claimed that they were fighting World War II to defeat the "Jewish conspiracy" against the German people. Nazi propaganda took written form in newspapers that were distributed to the troops but was also delivered directly in classes run by the Wehrmacht. A corps of men known as the National Socialist Leadership Officers indoctrinated soldiers in Nazi ideology through lectures and informal talks with frontline troops.

Some soldiers accepted Nazi anti-Semitism. According to Omer Bartov, in his book *Hitler's Army:*

*The front page of* Der Stürmer, *the Nazi Party's anti-Semitic newspaper, circa 1934. To promote party ideology, German soldiers received free copies.*

*Wehrmacht soldiers lead a group of Polish men to their execution.*

Private von Kaull believed that "international Jewry," already in control of the capitalist world, had taken "as a counterweight this proletarian insanity [communism]" as well: "Now these two powers of destruction have been sent to the field, now they are incited against Europe, against the heart of the West, in order to destroy Germany. . . . Such a huge battle has never before taken place on earth. It is . . . waged for the existence or downfall of Western man. . . . We must give our all to withstand this battle."[66]

## War Against the Subhumans

In addition to their hatred of Jews, the Nazis taught that all non-Germanic people, particularly the Slavic and Asiatic peoples of the Soviet Union, were inferior to pure German or "Aryan" people. In their propaganda they told their soldiers that the Slavs were less than human, pawns in the evil Jewish conspiracy, and that because they were such dangerous and implacable enemies, the only solution was to kill or enslave them all.

Few German soldiers seemed to question the necessity of absolute victory over the Soviet Union, including killing or enslaving the entire population. They were committed to a program of genocide that included the calculated, cold-blooded murder of men, women, and children. Nevertheless, Nazi soldiers saw themselves as normal, healthy family men who wanted to win the war, return home, and get on with their lives. In 1941, Karl Fuchs wrote a letter to his fiancée that indicates how the Germans regarded the Soviets:

> All you have to do is look at the Russian prisoners. Hardly ever do you see the face of a person who seems rational and

Over the last several centuries, nations have developed rules of war. Some of these are based on religious ideas, others on practicalities of the conduct of battle. For example, armies generally recognize a right to call a cease-fire to remove and bury dead soldiers and a right to safe conduct to engage in negotiations. And as long ago as the Middle Ages, it was understood that once they had surrendered, prisoners of war were not to be killed. Since the mid–nineteenth century, nations have worked together to write clear and binding rules of war.

The first major international agreement on the conduct of war was the Geneva Convention of 1864, which concerned the treatment of wounded soldiers. Then two meetings in the Netherlands in 1899 and 1907 produced the Hague Convention, which required that prisoners of war not be starved, enslaved, tortured, or killed. These rules were included in the 1929 Geneva Convention, which also covered the humane treatment of civilians. The Geneva Convention was signed by thirty-eight nations, including Germany, but the Soviet Union and Japan refused to sign.

Nazi soldiers generally obeyed the rules during the invasion of France, but they later participated in the arrest and deportation of French Jews to the death camps in Poland. On the eastern front, the Germans broke all the rules from the beginning. They knew that they would be safe from punishment for their atrocities only if they won the war; if they lost the war, many German soldiers thought that they and their families would be killed by any remaining Russians and Jews, so they killed as many as possible. The scale and brutality of their actions were so horrific that a new category of crime was developed after the war—crimes against humanity. According to the *Encyclopedia of the Third Reich*, these were defined in the Nuremberg war crimes trials as "murder, extermination, enslavement, deportation or other inhuman actions, which were perpetrated against any civilian population before or during the war, [and] persecution for political, racial, or religious reasons."

intelligent. They all look emaciated and the wild, half-crazy look in their eyes makes them appear like imbeciles. And these scoundrels, led by Jews and criminals, wanted to imprint their stamp on Europe, indeed on the world. Thank God that our Führer, Adolf Hitler, is preventing this from happening! . . . This war against these sub-human beings is about over. It's almost insulting when you consider that drunken Russian criminals have been let loose against us. We really let them have it! They are scoundrels, the mere scum of the earth. Naturally they are not a match for us German soldiers.[67]

## Race Hatred

The war crimes of the Nazis resulted from many factors—racial, political, economic, and military—some of which changed over the course of the war. One factor that did not change was Nazi hatred of non-Germanic people and especially Jews. Whether during a battle or after, whether as a soldier taken prisoner or a civilian, whether a man, woman, or child, Jews were killed by Nazi soldiers. They were shot, hanged, gassed, and worked or starved to death. Similar fates were often meted out to soldiers and civilians of Slavic and Asiatic ancestry.

There were important differences in the degree and extent of the war crimes the Nazis committed in Poland, western Europe, Yugoslavia, and the Soviet Union. In Poland, the first major military campaign of the war, tens of thousands of Jewish and Slavic civilians were killed, but the Nazis wanted to disguise this genocide. France and the United Kingdom, Poland's allies, declared war on Germany but did not launch an attack. German commanders thought that if their orders to kill civilians became widely known, an immediate attack would be more likely.

In contrast, when the Nazis invaded western Europe nine months later, they killed fewer civilians, partly because they saw the French, Belgians, Dutch, and Scandinavians as being more Germanic and partly because they did not want the United States to join the war.

The occupation of Yugoslavia in April 1941 by Germany and its allies was unique. Yugoslavia was made up of several regions with distinctive ethnic and religious characteristics, and serious conflicts among the Yugoslav peoples existed long before the occupation. This resulted in a complicated civil war and war of resistance to the occupation, with shifting alliances among the many nationalist, political, and religious groups. Most of the Nazis' atrocities in Yugoslavia occurred in the province of Serbia against both ethnic Serbs and Serbian Jews.

In their war with the Soviet Union, the Germans hardly tried to disguise the fact that they were killing Jews, Communists, and intellectuals and either not taking prisoners of war at all or treating them so harshly that they soon died. Though the SS was responsible for the worst atrocities, many in the Wehrmacht were also willing participants, especially in the mistreatment of POWs. The Russian war was not a blitzkrieg followed by an occupation, as in France, but a highly dynamic war lasting almost four years. In western Europe, the Germans wanted cooperation from the people of the occupied countries, but in the Soviet Union the Nazi policy was to exterminate or enslave the entire population and to destroy the Communist government. Thus, the war crimes committed on the eastern front were more widespread and severe than those on other fronts.

## A License to Kill

On May 13, 1941, the Wehrmacht High Command issued an order that became known as the Barbarossa Jurisdictional Decree. (Barbarossa was the code name for the invasion of the Soviet Union in June 1941.) The decree ordered that Soviet civilians captured for attacks on German soldiers would be punished at the discretion of local German commanders, who were encouraged to take "collective violent measures"[68] against any town or village from which attacks were launched. In practice, this meant that the soldiers of the Wehrmacht were authorized to round up civilians, even if they were not involved in attacks, and kill them. In some cases it meant that Wehrmacht soldiers murdered entire villages.

Hitler particularly feared that Communist political leaders, known as commissars, would lead Soviet POWs in rebellion. Therefore

*A German soldier executes a Jewish woman and her daughter in Ivanogorod, Ukraine, after forcing her to dig her own grave.*

Hitler told the commanders of the army, navy, and air force that

> the war against Russia will be such that it cannot be conducted in a knightly fashion. This struggle is one of ideologies and racial differences and will have to be conducted with unprecedented, unmerciful and unrelenting harshness. . . . I insist absolutely that my orders be executed without contradiction. The commissars are the bearers of ideologies directly opposed to National Socialism [Nazi ideology]. Therefore the commissars will be liquidated. German soldiers guilty of breaking international law . . . will be excused.[69]

Following Hitler's directive, on June 6, 1941, what became known as the Commissar Order was given to the senior commanders preparing for the invasion of the Soviet Union. It told them that all Communist Party commissars were to be executed.

## Crimes against Civilians

The rules of war allowed armies to battle guerrilla or partisan fighters and to execute partisans they captured because they were not part of a regular army. The Germans, however, classified anyone they wanted to get rid of as a partisan and any action against them as a battle. According to Omer Bartov:

> The extent to which this euphemism ["partisan battles"] was applied to what were in fact large-scale murder operations was demonstrated, for instance, by the report of the Wehrmacht commandant of Belorussia, who claimed to have shot 10,431 prisoners out of 10,940 taken in "battles with partisans" in October 1941 alone, all at the price of two German dead. Yet this was but one of many so-called "anti-partisan campaigns" which turned out to be outright massacres of unarmed civilians.[70]

Especially in the early days of the war, many Wehrmacht officers and enlisted men were repulsed by the killing of civilians. Some protested, and a few even refused to participate. In general, those who asked to be excluded from the firing squads were given other duties. But over time, virtually all soldiers in units assigned to kill civilians participated, probably as a result of group pressure. It became clear to German soldiers that these war crimes were not going to end because a few soldiers protested, and protesting cut men off from their fellow soldiers, the very people they would have to depend on in battle.

The German occupation of Serbia, a province of Yugoslavia, provides a clear example of the crimes of the Wehrmacht against civilians because its actions were documented in great detail. Serbia had a large Jewish population and several guerrilla groups that attacked the Germans. The head of the Wehrmacht High Command, Field Marshal Wilhelm Keitel, decreed that fifty to one hundred Communists should be killed for every German soldier who lost his life in the fighting in Serbia. The German commander in Serbia, General Franz Böhme, issued an order that further expanded the reprisals: "Ruthless measures must create a deterrent that will rapidly become known throughout Serbia. . . . All settlements from which or in whose vicinity German troops are fired on or in whose vicinity weapons or

## Concentration Camp Guards

If a soldier is someone who fights battles against other soldiers, then the guards at Nazi concentration camps were not soldiers. On the other hand, they were armed, wore uniforms, were members of Death's Head SS units, and were an integral part of the overall German military plan to rid Europe of "enemies of the German people."

German concentration camps were used in the mid-1930s to punish or "reeducate" political prisoners. As the Nazis solidified their power, more categories of people became subject to arrest: Jews, homosexuals, those judged to be "antisocial," and Jehovah's Witnesses. The first concentration camps were set up in abandoned factories, but soon camps were constructed specifically to house the rapidly expanding number of prisoners.

Political indoctrination was one early purpose of the camps, and some prisoners who adopted Nazi ideas were released. Increasingly, though, the camps were used for forced labor and extermination—prisoners were either killed shortly after arrival or worked to death. They were housed in primitive, unsanitary conditions, poorly clothed and fed, given little medical care, and worked from dawn to dark every day. Concentration camp guards beat, tortured, or killed prisoners for minor infractions or for no reason at all. Those whom the guards judged unable to work (the young, the old, and the sick) were killed outright by shooting, hanging, or poison gas. The bodies were buried in mass graves or cremated.

In early 1945, as Allied forces advanced into Germany and its occupied territories, many concentration camps were evacuated. Prisoners were then subjected to forced marches, and those who were too weak to keep up were shot. Food, shelter, and sanitary conditions in the new "collecting" camps were even worse than in the concentration camps. About one-third of prisoners died before the collecting camps were liberated.

munitions are found are to be burned to the ground."[71]

For example, in April 1941 in the town of Pančevo, two German soldiers were shot by partisans. In reprisal, thirty-six civilians were executed by Wehrmacht and SS soldiers on April 21 and 22, several by hanging, their bodies left exposed for several days.

The situation worsened in the summer of 1941. During July and August, thirty-two German soldiers died in Serbia as a result of partisan attacks, and the Wehrmacht executed over a thousand Communists and Jews in reprisal. One soldier wrote in a letter:

Can you receive Belgrade with your radio, every evening they broadcast German news

*A smiling Nazi poses for a photograph with a newly hanged Soviet citizen.*

at 8 and 10 p.m.? Maybe you will have a chance to hear it. But don't be shocked if the number of executed Communists and Jews happens to be announced. They are listed daily at the end of the news. Today a record was set! This morning 122 Communists and Jews were executed by us in Belgrade.[72]

The pace of the killing escalated in the following weeks. On October 8 an order was given to kill twenty-two hundred Jews housed at a camp in Belgrade. They were taken into the countryside by Wehrmacht units and shot. During the last two weeks of October over nine thousand Jews and other civilians were executed. As many as thirty thousand Serbian civilians were killed during the fall of 1941, including all the adult male Jews.

## The Role of the SS

The SS was given special responsibility for the murder of the Jews and other civilians. For example, Wehrmacht private P. Kluge described killings by the SS in Swiecie, Poland, on October 7, 1939:

We watched as a group consisting of a woman and three children, the children from about three to eight years of age, were led from a bus to a dug-out grave about 8 meters [26 feet] wide and 8 meters long. The woman was forced to climb down into this grave and carried her youngest child with her. The two other children were handed to her by two men of the execution squad. The woman had to lie flat on her stomach, with her face to the earth, her three children lined up in the same way to her left.

*Jewish men, women, and children await execution in a ravine near Rovno, Poland, in October 1942.*

Then four men stepped into the grave, placed the muzzles of their rifles about 30 cm [12 inches] from the backs of the necks, and shot the woman with her three children. I was then told by the Sturmbannführer [SS major] in charge to assist in shoveling dirt over the corpses. I obeyed the order and thus could observe from close up how the next groups of women and children were executed in a similar fashion. A total of 9–10 groups of women and children, each time four of them in the same mass grave.

About 200 *Wehrmacht* soldiers watched the shootings from a distance of about 30 meters [100 feet]. A little later a second bus drove up to the cemetery, carrying men with one woman among them. . . . A total of about 28 women, 25 men, and 10 children from 3–8 years old were executed on this morning.[73]

The most notorious atrocities of the SS were carried out by the *Einsatzgruppen*, which were mobile units attached to, but not under the command of, the Wehrmacht. The *Ein-*

*satzgruppen* were responsible for the deaths of at least nine hundred thousand persons in the Soviet Union. According to historian Richard Breitman:

Following just behind the German armies that invaded the Soviet Union in June 1941, four Einsatzgruppen—literally 'operational groups,' or battalions of policemen . . . —disposed of large numbers of Jews and other selected 'enemies' of the Third Reich, such as Communist officials and Gypsies. The company-sized subdivisions called Einsatzkommandos lined up their victims at the edge of trenches (or occasionally ravines) and shot them into their graves, or they placed their victims in the trenches, shot them there, and lined up the next group on top of the corpses. The Einsatzgruppen were at work for more than five months before the first operational extermination camp (at Chelmno [Poland]) began to liquidate Jews in gas chambers, and they carried out most of the killings in the first phase of the Holocaust in the Soviet territories.[74]

## Crimes against POWs

Nazi soldiers often refused to take prisoners, and instead executed wounded or surrendered soldiers. Incidents in which one or a few Allied soldiers were captured and killed often went unreported, but several larger incidents were well documented by survivors. The most famous of these occurred near the village of Malmédy, Belgium. On the afternoon of December 17, 1944, a convoy of American soldiers was ambushed by a unit of the *Waffen*-SS under the command of Colonel Joachim Peiper. When it became clear that their light weapons were no match for the tanks and machine guns of the SS, the Americans surrendered. Over one hundred American soldiers were disarmed and marched into a field. What happened next is described by one of the captured American soldiers, Private James Mattera:

> We all stood there with our hands up, when a German officer in a command car shot a [U.S.] medical officer and one enlisted man. They fell to the ground. Then the machine guns on the tanks opened up on the group of men and were killing everyone. We all lay on our stomachs, and every tank that came by would open up with machine guns on the group of men laying on the ground. This carried on about 30 minutes. . . .
>
> Then about three or four Germans came over to the group of men lying on the ground. Some officers and noncommissioned officers were shot in the head with pistols. After they left, the machine gunners opened up. . . . My buddies around me were getting hit and crying for help. I figured my best bet would be to make a break and run for my life.[75]

The SS executed eighty-six American soldiers that afternoon, but about forty either escaped or recovered from their wounds to tell the story. Colonel Peiper and his commander, General Sepp Dietrich, along with sixty-nine other German soldiers, were prosecuted after the war for their part in the incident. Twenty-five were given life sentences, and forty-two were condemned to death, but because of irregularities in the trial, the sentences were reduced—no Germans were executed for the massacre.

## Chaos and Revenge

Conditions were harsh for all POWs taken by the Germans, but in the Soviet Union the Wehrmacht was given great latitude and even encouragement to either kill outright or starve to death prisoners of war. Nearly 6 million Soviet soldiers were captured by the Germans. Almost 60 percent of them died in captivity. This death rate was unprecedented in modern warfare and derives from several factors.

First, the Germans executed POWs who were Communists, intellectuals, and Jews immediately upon capture. Military historians estimate that over half a million Russian POWs did not survive their first day as prisoners.

Second, the Germans did little to prepare for the huge numbers of Russian prisoners they captured and so killed them through deliberate neglect. POWs were routinely exposed to the elements with only their uniforms to keep them warm, given little or no medical attention, and fed very little. Bartov reports that the Wehrmacht was ordered to supply POWs "only with the most essential provisions," and to "feed them with the most primitive means."[76]

Guy Sajer describes the behavior of German soldiers in charge of Russian prisoners:

*American POWs lie murdered by German soldiers of Kampfgruppe Peiper at Malmédy, Belgium, in December 1944.*

The Russian prisoners were used to bury the dead [German soldiers], but it seemed they had taken to robbing the bodies. . . . I think . . . the poor fellows . . . were probably going over the bodies for something to eat. The rations we gave them were absurd—for example, one three-quart mess tin of weak soup for every four prisoners every twenty-four hours. On some days, they were given nothing but water.

Every prisoner caught robbing a German body was immediately shot. There were no official firing squads for these executions. An officer would simply shoot the offender on the spot, or hand him over to a couple of toughs who were regularly given this sort of job. Once, to my horror, I saw one of these thugs tying the hands of three prisoners to the bars of a gate. When his victims had been secured, he stuck a grenade into the pocket of one of their coats, pulled the pin, and ran for shelter. The three Russians, whose guts were blown out, screamed for mercy until the last moment.

Sajer goes on to explain that some soldiers in his unit confronted those who abused Russian prisoners. But the abusers were themselves escapees from the Russian Tomvos prison camp near Moscow, which they said was a death camp; there, German POWs too weak to work got no food at all; men who could work received one bowl of millet, a type of cereal, for every four workers; and if more prisoners were able to work than were needed, those not chosen

were simply killed: a favorite method of execution was to hammer an empty cartridge case into the nape of the prisoner's neck. It seemed that the Russians often distracted themselves with this type of sport.

I myself can well believe that the Russians were capable of this kind of cruelty. . . . But Russian excesses did not in any way excuse us for the excesses by our own side. War always reaches the depths of horror because of idiots who perpetrate terror from generation to generation under the pretext of vengeance.[77]

The crimes of Nazi soldiers led to new rules of war, an unprecedented number of

## German Soldiers as Historians

Some German soldiers who survived the war wrote memoirs of the war years, and others became historians. The accuracy of their writings about war crimes is questioned by American historian Omer Bartov in his book *Hitler's Army*.

"The popular collective memory of the war is one of a terrible event in which many people suffered and died as victims of an apocalypse beyond their control. . . . The facts are there for everyone to behold, but they are kept well apart from one's own experience and memory. [Wehrmacht veteran Werner] Paulsen will admit that the Germans too may have committed atrocities; but he had no part in them, nor had any of his colleagues. . . . Another historian, who had made a major contribution to our knowledge of Hitler's plans and preparations for the Vernichtungskrieg [war of annihilation] in the East, asks his (German) colleagues to identify with the German soldier, whose exploits he then describes with a great deal of pathos, only to proceed with a highly detached account of the 'final solution,' leaving the question of empathy with its victims to other, presumably Jewish historians."

An example of selective memory is the following excerpt from Basilius Streithofen, a German soldier who later became a priest. He is quoted in *Voices from the Third Reich*

by Johannes Steinhoff, Peter Peschel, and Dennis Showalter:

"I was sent to Holland for training. Next to our barracks was a large concentration camp, and Jews were always being moved in and out. One day we were asked if any of us wished to volunteer for a firing squad. In my room there were 16 or 17 of us, from everywhere in the Reich, and not one of us signed up, even though that would have meant extra rations. . . .

During the Warsaw uprising, we were shot at from a row of houses. In the evening we got together a detachment; early the next morning we made short work of the snipers. These are the sorts of things you can't forget. But we were soldiers, not butchers. In East Prussia, some Russians deserted to us. Our commander ordered us to shoot them. We told him, 'Lieutenant, shoot them yourself!' And he said, 'I insist that you obey my order.' We let them go."

Streithofen tells these stories as vindication of German soldiers, but he neglects to mention that even though his unit did not shoot the Jews, other German soldiers certainly did; that Jewish snipers fired at his unit during the Warsaw ghetto uprising because they knew they soon would be killed if they did not escape; and that his refusal to shoot Russian POWs on one occasion does not change the fact that over 3 million were killed by the Germans.

prosecutions for war crimes, and an enduring reputation for ruthless brutality that continues to haunt the German people.

## The Stress of Murder

How the Nazi soldiers reacted to their part in the killing of civilians and POWs varied greatly. According to SS lieutenant Albert Hartl:

There were people whose participation awakened in them the most evil impulses. For example, the head of one firing-squad made several hundred Jews of all ages, male and female, strip naked and run through a field into a wood. He then had them mown down with machine-gun fire. He even photographed the whole proceedings. . . . The [killings] also had the reverse effect on some of the SS men detailed to the firing-squads. These men were overcome with uncontrollable fits of crying and suffered health breakdowns.[78]

One soldier in the *Einsatzgruppen* recalled that

after the first wave of shootings it emerged that the men, particularly the officers, could not cope with the demands made on them. Many abandoned themselves to alcohol, many suffered nervous breakdowns and psychological illnesses; for example we had suicides and there were cases where some men cracked up and shot wildly around them and completely lost control. When this happened [SS head Heinrich] Himmler issued an order stating that any man who no longer felt able to take the psychological stresses should report to his superior officer.

These men were to be released from their current duties and would be detailed for other work back home.[79]

After the war, an SS sergeant maintained that there was nothing he could do to avoid participation in the killings, but his explanation suggests that saving face before his commanding officer, whose name was Leideritz, was as big a factor as coercion:

The reason I did not say to Leideritz that I could not take part in these things was that I was afraid that Leideritz and others would think I was a coward. I was worried that I would be affected adversely in some way in the future if I allowed myself to be seen as being too weak . . . that I was not as hard as an SS-Man ought to have been. . . .

I knew of no case and still know of no case today where one of us was sentenced to death because he did not want to take part in the execution of Jews. . . . I did not want to be seen in a bad light, and I thought that if I asked him to release me from having to take part in the executions . . . my chances of promotion would be spoilt.[80]

In fact, Ernst Ehlers and Franz Six, two SS officers interviewed after the war, said that when they asked to be transferred away from direct participation in the killings, their requests were granted and they suffered no disadvantages in terms of assignment or promotion. Though a few individual commanders may have denied requests for transfer, the evidence indicates that in most cases, participation in the killings was voluntary.

# CHAPTER 6

# "Stand and Die": The Defense of the Fatherland

In the final phase of the war, Nazi soldiers found themselves battling the Allies throughout occupied Europe. The United States entered the war after the Japanese attack on Pearl Harbor on December 7, 1941. In July 1943 the Allies landed in Sicily, and the following September they landed on the Italian mainland. Then came the Allied invasion of northern France on June 6, 1944, which was followed by Allied landings in the south of France in August. The western Allies fought their way through village after village in Italy and France, advancing toward Berlin, while the Soviets advanced on Berlin from the east. Hitler's orders were that a German soldier's duty was "to stand and die in his defenses."[81]

In Normandy, German soldiers fought and died on the beaches, in the fields and hedgerows, in the streets, and in the forests. As they retreated they were forced to defend their own homeland, fighting on the streets of their own cities, which had been bombed for months by the Americans and the British. It all ended in May 1945, the führer dead, the Reich collapsed, and Berlin overrun by Soviet forces bent on revenge against German soldiers—many of whom fled westward in the desperate hope of being taken prisoner by the Americans or British instead of falling into the hands of the Russians.

## D Day: June 6, 1944

The Allied landing on the beaches of Normandy in northern France was the largest amphibious assault in history. In a single day, 23,400 Allied paratroopers and 130,000 infantry soldiers landed on beaches code-named Omaha, Utah, Gold, Juno, and Sword. Facing this formidable invading force the Nazis had twenty-four battle ready divisions in France, but relatively few of these troops were near the invasion sites in Normandy. All German units suffered from shortages of fuel and other supplies. The Allies had complete air superiority, with nearly 17,000 aircraft to under 200 for the Germans. By June 18, the Allies had landed over 600,000 soldiers and nearly 100,000 vehicles.

Some of the German soldiers who fought at Normandy were veterans of the desert campaign in North Africa or of the Russian front. In contrast to these seasoned soldiers were the old men, teenage boys, and men with chronic illnesses the Wehrmacht had to resort to using. Many had no combat experience and little training. The Germans also used conscripted foreign troops in the fighting at Normandy. These included men from France, Italy, Croatia, Hungary, Romania, Poland, Finland, Estonia, Latvia, Lithuania, North Africa, and the Soviet Union. These troops were often unreliable and tended to surrender quickly. As one German officer said, "We are asking rather a lot if we expect Russians to fight in France for Germany against the Americans."[82]

By D day, German soldiers in the west were no longer using the highly mobilized blitzkrieg tactics they had used in the beginning of the war. In anticipation of an Allied invasion, the Nazis had built a massive system of fortifications along the northern coast of France called the Atlantic Wall. The Atlantic Wall consisted of steel-reinforced concrete bunkers, machine-gun pits, artillery pieces, observation towers, radar posts, underground troop shelters, and trenches fortified with barbed wire and mines. Beach obstacles such as booby traps, mines, and wooden posts and steel structures also were installed to prevent Allied landing craft from coming ashore.

Stretching 1,670 miles along the coastline from the Netherlands to Spain, the Atlantic Wall took four years to build, but it failed to prevent Allied landings at Normandy in June 1944. In fact, it held up the British and American troops for less than a day at Omaha Beach—and for less than an hour at Utah, Gold, Juno, and Sword Beaches. Noted D day historian Stephen Ambrose calls the Atlantic Wall "one of the greatest blunders in military history," explaining that because "there was absolutely no depth to the Atlantic Wall, once it had been penetrated, even if only by a kilometer, it was useless. Worse than useless, because the *Wehrmacht* troops manning the Atlantic Wall east and west of the invasion area were immobile, incapable of rushing to the sound of the guns."[83]

*By 1945, the German army was forced to draft old men and adolescent boys to compensate for the staggering losses incurred during the war.*

## On the Beaches

Second Lieutenant Arthur Jahnke of the 919th German Infantry Regiment, on seeing wave after wave of Allied soldiers and vehicles come ashore at Utah Beach, lamented, "It looks as though God and the world have forsaken us."[84] The Germans had been under heavy air bombardment all night, with Allied paratroopers landing in their midst. The German High Command had at first disbelieved the reports coming from the front of these massive Allied landings, and German soldiers were not given clearance to engage in battle until it was too late to effectively counter the invasion.

German frontline troops and commanders had been promised one thousand aircraft, but they were nowhere to be seen as the Allies waded ashore. Believing that this attack was a diversion for the real invasion, which they thought would be at Calais, Hitler and the German High Command were reluctant to divert the *Luftwaffe* from the Calais area.

Under attack from the invading Allied forces, many German soldiers felt abandoned, wondering where their air cover was. Samuel Mitcham Jr. recounts a grim joke that circulated among German ground troops: "If the airplane above you is camouflaged, it's British, if it's silver, it's American; and if it isn't there at all, it's the *Luftwaffe!*"[85] As Paul Carell writes, German soldiers "lay on their stomachs, their faces pressed into the ground, waiting for the end. Those are minutes that even the most hardboiled soldier never forgets. He feels forsaken by every one, alone, entirely alone with his fear and the reality of war—a war which, on those occasions, he curses a thousand times."[86]

## In the Hedgerows

Beyond the beaches at Normandy lay hedgerow country—thousands of small fields enclosed by mounds of dirt, which were topped by dense

*Allied planes like the P-51 Mustang fighter (right) had swept Germany's air force from the skies by 1944–45.*

thickets of hawthorn, brambles, vines, and trees. With drainage ditches on either side, these walls and hedges ranged up to fifteen feet in height and were as difficult to penetrate as small forts. Called *bocage* by the French, the hedgerows had been used as natural fortifications since Roman times.

The Germans dug in behind these hedgerows and cut small slits for their MG-42 machine guns. This gave the Germans what one American called "absolute protection. You couldn't see them as they fired."[87] The Germans would allow their enemy to enter a field and then cut them down with mortar and artillery fire. In the hedgerows, the Germans used *Panzerfausts* against the Allied tanks. The Americans blasted holes in the hedgerows with TNT to open a path for their Sherman tanks. German snipers hid on wooden platforms in treetops and used flashless gunpowder to conceal their positions.

Hitler's orders to Field Marshals Rommel and Rundstedt, the supreme commanders at Normandy, were that "every man shall fight and die where he stands."[88] German soldiers fought stubbornly and with great skill in the hedgerows, but morale was low and many were ready to admit defeat. As one American soldier put it, the German soldiers he encountered in the hedgerows were "so happy to be captured that all they could do was giggle."[89]

Others were determined to comply with Hitler's orders to die fighting, such as the fanatical captain in charge of Lance Corporal Josef Häger's unit. Häger was an eighteen-year-old machine gunner with the 716th Infantry Division, fighting in the hedgerows behind Sword Beach. He and nineteen other men were pinned down in a trench before a small bunker, under intense enemy fire from machine guns, mortars, and rifles. Inside the bunker, the captain was firing a machine gun at the enemy. He refused to let Häger and the other men inside

for cover from the shelling. Only when a British tank began to advance on them did the captain allow the men inside the bunker.

The hot, dark, and noisy bunker was filled with dead and dying men as Häger and the others rushed inside. There was no room to sit or even turn around. Then the British fired a flamethrower toward the bunker. As the temperature rose, the metal faring of the air shaft became white-hot. The men inside began to suffocate, as the only opening in the bunker was the port through which the captain continued to fire the machine gun. Häger and the others, including a young lieutenant, began to plead with the captain to surrender, but he refused, saying, "It's out of the question. We're going to fight our way out."[90]

Facing certain death, the men defiantly pulled out the bolts of their rifles and threw them down. Corporal Häger, too, pulled the locking pin on his machine gun and threw it down. As Cornelius Ryan relates in his book *The Longest Day*, "Men began to collapse from the heat. Knees buckling, heads lolling, they remained in a partly upright position; they could not fall to the floor. The young lieutenant continued to plead with the captain, but to no avail. No one could get to the door, because the aperture was next to it and the captain was there with his machine gun."[91]

Finally, the captain stopped firing long enough to turn around and look at the gasping men inside the bunker with him. Then, resigned to the hopelessness of the situation, he ordered the door opened and allowed the men to stumble outside, where they surrendered to the British.

## D Day Casualties and Prisoners

The casualties for D day were staggering on both sides. No accurate records were kept of German casualties, but official estimates range from 4,000

# July 20, 1944

In 1944, a group of dissatisfied German generals entered into a conspiracy to assassinate Adolf Hitler and seek an armistice with the Allies. On July 20, 1944, Count Claus Schenk von Stauffenberg, a colonel on Hitler's staff, placed a briefcase containing a plastic explosive beneath the table at a staff meeting. The detonation killed three members of Hitler's staff but left Hitler only slightly wounded.

Reactions to the failed assassination attempt varied. Many Germans, soldiers and civilians alike, took the fact that the attempt on the führer's life had failed as proof that Hitler was invincible and had been chosen by God to lead the German people to their rightful destiny as masters of Europe. Other German soldiers, disillusioned by a führer who was leading them to annihilation, were sorry the attempt failed. Martin Pöppel was recovering from combat wounds at a German base hospital in Paris at the time. In his book *Heaven and Hell* he writes:

"In the hospital we hear about the attempt to assassinate the Führer. Although there are SS officers here as well, we all discuss things quite openly. They are frontline soldiers the same as us, not the Black SS. . . . Even the SS men reckon that if we manage to win the war, the party will have to be dealt with afterwards. Most of them don't agree with the assassination attempt, but the prevailing opinion is that the Generals are at fault for relinquishing their famed leadership qualities to the so-called 'Greatest Military Leader of all Time.' How did the poor buggers at the front, and the exhausted civilian population at home, deserve to be led so badly?"

*Adolf Hitler shows Italian dictator Benito Mussolini the bomb damage at Hitler's retreat, the Wolf's Lair, after the failed July 20 assassination attempt.*

to 9,000 dead, missing, and wounded. On the beaches, trenches were filled with German soldiers who had been killed by Allied strafing and artillery fire. As German soldiers fell back from the beaches and hedgerows, they were unable to carry their wounded and had to leave them behind, in the hands of the Allies. German prisoners were gathered on the beaches and transported across the Channel to captivity in England for the duration of the war.

Within the first ten weeks after D day, 200,000 Germans were taken prisoner and at least 50,000 were killed. By September, the number of German soldiers taken prisoner had risen to 360,000, and the number killed had reached 250,000.

## On the Streets

German soldiers fought tenaciously in the streets of cities across occupied Europe and their own homeland as they tried to hold their ground. The fortified town of Monte Cassino saw bitter fighting during the Germans' struggle to keep the Allies from advancing through Italy; between January and May 1944 the Germans held out during four separate battles before finally being forced to withdraw their defense of the city. In Caen, France—which the British had originally planned to take on D day—the Germans held out for six weeks. Similarly, in Budapest, Hungary, German troops fought for seven weeks before surrendering to the Allies.

In Arnhem, Holland, the fighting was particularly intense. Battles raged through the streets, with snipers firing from windows of homes, shops, and the tower of a local church. Neither side could be sure who they would encounter as they rounded the corner of a building or made their way through a hedge. The Germans and British fought hand-to-hand with knives and bayonets. Battles were

waged literally room by room and house by house. SS squad leader Alfred Ringsdorff, a veteran of the Russian front, was forced by British marksmen on the streets of Arnhem to take refuge inside a house with his men. There, they smashed the windows and began firing on the British, who took cover in the house next door. Ringsdorff recalls the ensuing firefight: "The British shooting was deadly. We could hardly show ourselves. They aimed for the head, and men began to fall beside me, each one with a small, neat hole through the forehead."[92]

Ringsdorff and his men then charged the British-occupied house next door, where he recounts: "The fighting was cruel. . . . We pushed them back room by room, yard by yard, suffering terrible losses."[93] Ringsdorff ordered his men to keep up a constant shower of grenades against the British to drive them out of the house:

> Only in this way were we able to gain ground and continue our advance. But I certainly had not expected when I came from Germany [to Arnhem] to find myself suddenly engaged in bitter fighting in a restricted area. This was a harder battle than any I had fought in Russia. It was constant, close-range, hand-to-hand fighting. The English were everywhere. The streets, for the most part, were narrow, sometimes not more than fifteen feet wide, and we fired at each other from only yards away. We fought to gain inches, cleaning out one room after the other. It was absolute hell![94]

## In the Ardennes

What the Germans called the Ardennes Offensive and the Allies called the Battle of the Bulge

*Young German soldiers walk past a burning U.S. Army vehicle during the Battle of the Bulge in Belgium in December 1944.*

was the Germans' last great offensive of the war. The Ardennes region, located primarily in Belgium, consists of thick forests. The Germans launched their offensive on December 17, 1944, in snowy weather that initially grounded Allied planes. On this date, more than a quarter million German soldiers attacked eighty-three thousand Americans along the eighty-five-mile-long Ardennes front in an attempt to cut Allied forces in two and prevent them from advancing farther into Germany.

The Germans were armed with MP-44 automatic assault rifles, newly developed G-43 semiautomatic rifles, and *Panzerfausts* in the Ardennes Offensive. They also used a multibarreled rocket launcher called a *Nebelwerfer*, first used on the eastern front, which fired projectiles with such a loud screech that American soldiers called them "screaming meemies."

Winter conditions made fighting in the Ardennes a nightmare for both sides. Troops had to trudge through snow that was sometimes waist deep. Bodies of fallen comrades froze and their corpses had to be carried through the snow. The Germans enjoyed initial success due to the element of surprise—they had not been expected to strike under such poor weather conditions and in such densely wooded terrain.

But their supplies, as in every other campaign of the war, were inadequate, whereas the Allies had seemingly endless sources of fresh equipment and reinforcements. Hitler was determined to continue fighting in the Ardennes long after the battle had been lost and consequently expended the last of the Third Reich's reserves of troops and weapons. During the six weeks of fighting, German casualties totaled one hundred thousand dead, missing, and wounded; also lost were nearly all the tanks and aircraft committed to the campaign.

## In Defense of Their Homeland

In March 1942, the Allies began systematic air bombardment of large industrial towns in Germany. In May 1942, the city of Cologne was the target of the first "thousand-bomber raid"—the largest air raid in history up to that time—which left 469 Germans dead, 5,027 wounded, and 45,132 homeless. Air raids over Hamburg in the last week of July 1943 killed 44,600 civilians and 800 servicemen and reduced half the city—including 227,330 homes—to rubble.

Dresden, bombed in February 1945, was laid to ruin. Death-toll estimates range from 35,000 to 75,000 people, many of them refugees from other bombed-out cities. By 1945, over half the houses in Germany had been destroyed by Allied bombing.

Berlin was a prime target for air raids. On a secret mission to visit the führer in April 1943, Hans Luck observed: "The city presented a picture of destruction, many of the houses were now just ruins and the faces of the once busy Berliners were gray. One could see that they no longer believed in the 'Final Victory' of Hitler and Goebbels, though no one dared say as much; the danger of denunciation was too great."[95] In the final months of the war, morale in Berlin crumbled as the "heart of the Reich" was bombed almost continually by the Americans and the British. The *Luftwaffe*, outnumbered and short on fuel and pilots, was unable to mount an effective defense of the homeland.

One by one, German cities fell to advancing Allied troops. In late April 1945, Siegfried Knappe's artillery division was trying to hold the bridgeheads east of Berlin to

## The Real Heroes of Germany

Lieutenant Martin Pöppel was sent to recuperate from combat wounds at home in a suburb of Munich during the summer of 1944. In his book *Heaven and Hell*, he recounts his feelings when he and fellow soldiers on leave witnessed Allied planes bombing Munich by daylight.

"We leave each other depressed, thinking not just of those poor people there, but everywhere. Almost every night, and now by day as well, hurrying to the bunkers with a few personal belongings, suffering the terri-

ble explosions, the infernal noise all around, the trembling, waiting for death at any moment. Aren't the old men, the women and children the real heroes? And they can't even open their mouths to cry out in fear, in case the air raid warden is still a committed Nazi who might report them. No, it's better by far to be out there, back at the front."

Allied bombing of German cities during World War II destroyed 3.37 million residences, injured 917,000 people, and killed between 600,000 and 1 million German civilians.

keep the Soviets from overtaking the capital of the Third Reich. Knappe describes what it was like to be under Russian fire inside a city:

> We had to drive through continuous artillery fire, now including heavy artillery. It was a feeling akin to terror, with heavy artillery shells exploding all around us, and roof tiles, window frames, and chunks of street pavement flying through the air. It seemed as if the whole world were exploding around us. Artillery fire in a city is much more frightening than it is in the open. Whenever a shell hit something above us and exploded there, it sprayed shrapnel and fragments of whatever it hit all over.[96]

*As the war nears an end, three Germans man a machine-gun position in the Westwall, part of Germany's national defense line.*

# Running from the Red Army

As the Third Reich was in the final stages of collapse, millions of German soldiers fled the eastern front and the advancing Red Army. In *The Last 100 Days*, author John Toland describes the soldiers' state of fear as they tried to reach "American sanctuary." Toland recounts the panic that broke out among an SS division in Austria at the sight of a single Russian tank.

"Many [German soldiers from the eastern front] were funneling into Enns, Austria, hoping to cross the river into the lines of the U.S. 65th Division.

Late in the afternoon [of May 8, 1945], lines of weary Germans from the 12th SS Panzer Division approached the bridge, where a heavy log barricade had only been cleared enough to let a single truck squeeze through. Someone cried, *'Russky!'* and there was a stampede toward the bridge. Trucks ground into the surging mass of men. At least fifteen were killed instantly and countless others mangled. The bridge approach was hopelessly jammed and the terrified Germans fanned out along the river bank for a mile, shouting, *'Russky! Russky! Russky!'*

A squat medium tank clanked toward the bridge. A Red Army lieutenant stood in the turret, laughing at the sight of 6000 men frantically scrambling to escape his single gun."

---

Seventy-five thousand German troops defended Berlin in the final weeks of the war—including boys as young as twelve and housewives who were trained to fire *Panzerfausts*. The city had already been 75 percent destroyed by round-the-clock British and American air bombardment. The defenders had few tanks or guns and little ammunition, fuel, or food as Russian shelling turned the city into a wasteland. Altogether, five hundred thousand lives were lost in defense of Berlin.

## The Death of Hitler

German cities lay in ruins. Rations for civilians were at starvation level. Berlin was besieged by 1.25 million Russian soldiers. The Third Reich collapsing around him, Hitler committed suicide along with his bride, Eva Braun, in his private bunker in Berlin on April 30, 1945. Their corpses were rolled in a carpet, doused with gasoline, and burned so that they would not fall into the hands of the Russians.

Knappe learned of Hitler's death from his commander. Like many other German soldiers, Knappe was stunned by the news:

For some reason, it had never occurred to me that Hitler would commit suicide. If he planned to commit suicide, why had he not done it long ago, when it was obvious that the war was lost? Why had so many people had to die so senselessly, right up to the moment the Russians were knocking at the bunker door? Such selfishness was unbelievable to me.[97]

Alexander Stahlberg, who had been involved in a July 20, 1944, attempt on Hitler's life, felt relief at the news Hitler was dead. He writes in his memoir, "It is not easy to describe what went through my mind at that moment. 'Thank God!—I feel as if I have been saved from death myself.' The tension and burden of more than nine months since 20 July 1944 have suddenly slipped away. And the end of the war is near."[98]

## Unconditional Surrender

German soldiers fighting on the war's final front in defense of Berlin knew their choices had narrowed to death or captivity. Many feared being taken prisoner by the Soviets, who treated German soldiers and civilians savagely in retaliation for German atrocities committed in Russia. Some remained and fought to the end, while others fled toward the oncoming American and British armies to surrender to them. Millions of German soldiers—seventy thousand in Berlin alone—were captured by the Soviets in the final days of the war.

The Wehrmacht chief of staff, General Alfred Jodl, signed an unconditional surrender on May 7, 1945. Knappe, who had been captured by Russian troops on May 2, writes of his feelings immediately after the surrender:

> Being captured had always been a real possibility for all of us, but surrendering our country . . . I felt stunned now, almost

*German soldiers, fearing retribution from Soviet troops, often walked great distances to surrender to American, Canadian, or British forces.*

as if I were in someone else's bad dream. The war had shattered my life and left only a deep void. Home and a normal life were things I would probably never know again. I had to learn to adjust to our total defeat and my status as a prisoner of the Russians. It was a feeling of complete desperation.[99]

The desperation Knappe felt after the surrender was in sharp contrast to the euphoric pride he and other German soldiers felt early in the war. For many German soldiers, whether seasoned veterans or new recruits, the defeat of the Fatherland was a shattering experience that was followed by years of captivity as prisoners of war of the victorious Allies.

# Aftermath

Approximately 18 million men served as Nazi soldiers during the course of World War II. A significant number of them—3.8 million—were killed during the war. Millions became prisoners of war. Others were arrested, charged with war crimes, and executed. Many committed suicide rather than face trial or execution. Today, the German view of Nazi soldiers is as varied as it was during the war. Many people just want to forget the war and the Nazi era—but there are those who will never forget.

## Prisoners of War and War Criminals

Of the 9 million German soldiers serving in the Wehrmacht in 1945, more than 7 million became prisoners of war. More than 4 million were taken prisoner by the Americans and British shortly before and after the surrender. All German POWs still being held by the western Allies were freed by 1948, but three hundred thousand had died as a result of mistreatment while in American and French captivity. The death rate among the 6 million Germans taken captive by the Russians over the course of the war was much higher, with well over half perishing. Approximately fifty thousand were convicted as war criminals and spent up to ten years at hard labor in Russian prison camps before their release. Among these was Colonel Hans Luck, sentenced to five years' labor in the coal mines of the Caucasus Mountains.

Conditions for German POWs in Russia were deplorable. Prisoners slept on straw mattresses on board bunks wide enough for two men but frequently holding up to six. Rations were barely at the subsistence level. Escape attempts rarely succeeded—the prison camps were deep inside Russia, and prisoners who were recaptured were brutally beaten and put in solitary confinement for weeks. In France, too, German prisoners were often brutalized by guards and townspeople who wanted to get even for the occupation. Up to twenty thousand Germans died clearing minefields in France—a direct violation of the 1929 Geneva Convention, which prohibited use of POWs for dangerous work.

At war crimes trials, most notably at Nuremberg, Germany, hundreds of prominent Nazis were sentenced to death by hanging or to imprisonment ranging from ten years to life. Many Nazis committed suicide, either in the closing hours of the war or while awaiting trial or sentencing.

## Emigration

After the war, many former Nazi soldiers emigrated to other countries. Otto Friedrich writes that for those whose homes had been reduced to rubble in Berlin and other cities, there was little desire "to return to the hollowed-out, filled-in relic of the city they once knew."[100] Many Germans wanted to get out of the Russian-occupied zone of Germany and away from

Communist rule. After his release from a Russian prison camp, Major Siegfried Knappe struggled to get out of East Germany with his wife and two young sons. Finally, in 1955, he and his family emigrated to the United States.

## Remembering Nazi Germany

How do Germans look back on the war and the Nazi era? Bernt Engelmann, a *Luftwaffe* radio operator, was arrested by the Gestapo in 1944 for his participation in resistance activities. In his book *In Hitler's Germany: Daily Life in the Third Reich*, Engelmann describes the various ways in which Germans recall their country under Nazi rule:

Those years are reflected very differently in the memories of Germans who lived through them. Much depends on how each individual viewed the Nazi regime at the time and how he chose to respond to it: as a blindly loyal supporter; as an opportunistic fellow traveler who saw only his own gain; as a docile, apolitical citizen, who obeyed the authorities and did what he considered his duty; as one who kept quiet and shut his eyes but was "privately against it all"; as an innocent victim; as someone who resisted the regime as best he could, cautiously rather than passively; or even as someone who repeatedly risked his life by resisting boldly and actively.[101]

*High-ranking Nazi leaders on trial for war crimes at Nuremberg, Germany, in 1946.*

Former Wehrmacht officer Siegfried Knappe, in contemplation at a Russian prison camp, questioned the morality of his country's actions during the war. In his memoir *Soldat*, he writes about his realization that he and his fellow soldiers had blindly accepted the ideas of Hitler and the Nazi Party:

I spent most of those first three weeks going over Germany's experience of the previous six years. Where had we gone so wrong? . . . It was only now beginning to dawn on me that our treatment of other nations had been arrogant—that the only justification we had felt necessary was our own need.

As these things all went through my mind, I began to realize that I should have thought them through at the time of their occurrence—but I was a soldier, and a soldier does not question the orders of his superiors. I had unquestioningly accepted the brutal philosophy that might makes right; the arrogance of our national behavior had not even occurred to me at the time. Although such blind obedience was probably the only military way to keep soldiers focused on the task at hand, the realization that I had allowed myself to become a nonthinking cog in Hitler's military machine depressed me now. . . . In retrospect, I realized that I—and countless others like me—had helped Hitler start and fight a world war of conquest that had left tens of millions of people dead and destroyed our own country. I wondered now whether I would ever have questioned these things if we had won the war. I had to conclude that it was unlikely. This was a lesson taught by defeat, not by victory.[102]

Many Germans today do not want to be reminded of their country's role in the war. A schoolteacher in Germany describes the resentment she encounters when teaching about this period of history:

At school, some of the students are very interested in this period. . . . The persecution of the Jews, students are very interested in that, although there are many other aspects. But parents soon start to complain. They ask me to let this period of history rest, to let it be. They say you can't go on talking forever about those

*This Nazi soldier's face clearly shows the horrors of war in Belgium in 1944.*

things, and that I bring up only the negative side. They say there were also good things about Hitler. Those years weren't all that bad. . . . They mention building the autobahns and solving the unemployment problem, that crime wasn't as serious a problem then as it is today. A typical complaint is that I don't talk about what the Allies did [to the Germans]. "How about Dresden?" So the parents have been protesting, saying I should stop.[103]

But Verena Groth, a half-Jewish woman who lived in Germany during the war, condemns former Nazis who want to hang on to their glory days:

Before the war, many had no big careers or were nothing special themselves. Then they had careers as being true [Nazi] Party members. And in 1945, the career was over and they were only average citizens. Now they cling to this time. It was their golden age. They simply do not admit that they erred, or more carefully put, that they were seduced. . . . They've LEARNED NOTHING in forty years. They remain as stupid as they were.[104]

The social and legal situation in Germany early in the twenty-first century is in many ways the reverse of conditions during the Nazi era. Germany now has some of the strongest laws in the world against anti-Semitism and other forms of bigotry, and the majority of the population favors peace and tolerance. A small minority, however—some of them former soldiers of the Third Reich—still think Hitler was right. Though neo-Nazi groups are officially banned, hate crimes such as defacing concentration camp memorials and synagogues still occur in Germany.

# Notes

## Introduction: Who Were the Nazi Soldiers?

1. Siegfried Knappe and Ted Brusaw, *Soldat*. New York: Dell, 1992, p. xi.
2. Quoted in Stephen G. Fritz, *Frontsoldaten: The German Soldier in World War II*. Lexington: University Press of Kentucky, 1995, pp. 158–59.
3. Quoted in John Lukacs, *Five Days in London: May 1940*. New Haven, CT: Yale University Press, 1999, pp. 16–17.
4. Martin Pöppel, *Heaven and Hell: The War Diary of a German Paratrooper*. New York: Hippocrene Books, 1988, p. 11.

## Chapter 1: Initiation into Battle

5. Guy Sajer, *Forgotten Soldier*. Washington, DC: Brassey's (US), 1990, p. 162.
6. Heinz Guderian, *Achtung-Panzer!: The Development of Armoured Forces, Their Tactics, and Operational Potential*, 1937. London: Arms and Armour, 1992, p. 23.
7. Alexander Stahlberg, *Bounden Duty: The Memoirs of a German Officer, 1932–1945*. London: Brassey's (UK), 1990, p. 146.
8. Quoted in Hans von Luck, *Panzer Commander: The Memoirs of Colonel Hans von Luck*. New York: Dell, 1989, p. 39.
9. Luck, *Panzer Commander*, p. 27.
10. Heinz Guderian, *Panzer Leader*. New York: Da Capo, 1996, p. 68.
11. Luck, *Panzer Commander*, pp. 28–29.
12. Knappe and Brusaw, *Soldat*, pp. 153–55.
13. Quoted in Horst Fuchs Richardson and Dennis Showalter, eds., *Sieg Heil!: War Letters of Tank Gunner Karl Fuchs, 1937–1941*. Hamden, CT: Archon Books, 1987, p. 43.

14. Knappe and Brusaw, *Soldat*, pp. 160–61.
15. Knappe and Brusaw, *Soldat*, p. 172.
16. Stahlberg, *Bounden Duty*, p. 132.
17. Knappe and Brusaw, *Soldat*, p. 155.
18. Knappe and Brusaw, *Soldat*, p. 174.
19. Luck, *Panzer Commander*, p. 57.

## Chapter 2: Army of Occupation: Training and Waiting

20. Knappe and Brusaw, *Soldat*, pp. 190–91.
21. Luck, *Panzer Commander*, p. 56.
22. Quoted in Richardson and Showalter, *Sieg Heil!*, p. 73.
23. Pöppel, *Heaven and Hell*, p. 115.
24. Knappe and Brusaw, *Soldat*, pp. 193–94.
25. Pöppel, *Heaven and Hell*, p. 93.
26. Luck, *Panzer Commander*, pp. 51–52.
27. Quoted in Claire Chevrillon, *Code Name Christiane Clouet: A Woman in the French Resistance*. College Station: Texas A&M University Press, 1995, p. 21.
28. Pöppel, *Heaven and Hell*, p. 115.
29. Knappe and Brusaw, *Soldat*, pp. 195–97.
30. Chevrillon, *Code Name Christiane Clouet*, p. 18.
31. Luck, *Panzer Commander*, p. 61.
32. Quoted in Chevrillon, *Code Name Christiane Clouet*, p. 52.
33. Quoted in David Pryce-Jones, *Paris in the Third Reich: A History of the German Occupation, 1940–1944*. New York: Holt, Rinehart and Winston, 1981, p. 243.
34. Quoted in Pryce-Jones, *Paris in the Third Reich*, pp. 198–99.

## Chapter 3: The Eastern Front

35. Quoted in Fritz, *Frontsoldaten*, p. 119.
36. Knappe and Brusaw, *Soldat*, p. 228.
37. Sajer, *Forgotten Soldier*, pp. 327–29.

38. Knappe and Brusaw, *Soldat*, p. 229.
39. Knappe and Brusaw, *Soldat*, p. 230.
40. Quoted in Fritz, *Frontsoldaten*, p. 110.
41. Knappe and Brusaw, *Soldat*, pp. 233–34.
42. Sajer, *Forgotten Soldier*, p. 28.
43. Quoted in Fritz, *Frontsoldaten*, p. 111.
44. Quoted in Fritz, *Frontsoldaten*, p. 111.
45. Sajer, *Forgotten Soldier*, p. 345.
46. Knappe and Brusaw, *Soldat*, p. 233.
47. Sajer, *Forgotten Soldier*, p. 316.
48. Quoted in Fritz, *Frontsoldaten*, pp. 65–67.
49. Fritz, *Frontsoldaten*, pp. 239–40.

## Chapter 4: The Afrika Korps: "To the Last Bullet"

50. Ronald Lewin, *The Life and Death of the Afrika Korps*. New York: Quadrangle/The New York Times, 1977, p. 11.
51. Desmond Young, *Rommel: The Desert Fox*. New York: Quill, 1978, p. 118.
52. Heinz Werner Schmidt, *With Rommel in the Desert*. New York: Ballantine, 1967, p. 178.
53. Luck, *Panzer Commander*, p. 147.
54. Schmidt, *With Rommel in the Desert*, p. 165.
55. Schmidt, *With Rommel in the Desert*, p. 61.
56. Luck, *Panzer Commander*, p. 95.
57. Schmidt, *With Rommel in the Desert*, p. 46.
58. Kenneth Macksey, *Rommel: Battles and Campaigns*. New York: Mayflower, 1979, p. 113.
59. Schmidt, *With Rommel in the Desert*, pp. 114–15.
60. Luck, *Panzer Commander*, p. 101.
61. Schmidt, *With Rommel in the Desert*, p. 184.
62. Lewin, *The Life and Death of the Afrika Korps*, p. 196.
63. Luck, *Panzer Commander*, p. 120.
64. Quoted in Richard Collier and the Editors of Time-Life Books, *The War in the Desert*. Alexandria, VA: Time-Life Books, 1977, p. 195.
65. Quoted in Lewin, *The Life and Death of the Afrika Korps*, p. 36.

## Chapter 5: War Crimes

66. Quoted in Omer Bartov, *Hitler's Army: Soldiers, Nazis, and War in the Third Reich*. New York: Oxford University Press, 1992, p. 161.
67. Quoted in Richardson and Showalter, *Sieg Heil!*, pp. 122–23.
68. Quoted in Christian Zentner and Friedemann Bedürftig, eds., *The Encyclopedia of the Third Reich*. New York: Da Capo, 1997, p. 66.
69. Quoted in William L. Shirer, *The Rise and Fall of the Third Reich: A History of Nazi Germany*. New York: Simon and Schuster, 1960, p. 830.
70. Bartov, *Hitler's Army*, pp. 84–85.
71. Quoted in Hamburg Institute for Social Research, *The German Army and Genocide: Crimes Against War Prisoners, Jews, and Other Civilians in the East, 1939–1944*. New York: New Press, 1999, p. 52.
72. Quoted in Hamburg Institute, *The German Army and Genocide*, p. 50.
73. Quoted in Hamburg Institute, *The German Army and Genocide*, p. 26.
74. Richard Breitman, *Official Secrets: What the Nazis Planned, What the British and Americans Knew*. New York: Hill and Wang, 1998, p. 4.
75. Quoted in *Reporting World War II: American Journalism: Part Two, 1944–1946*. New York: Library of America, 1995, p. 581.
76. Bartov, *Hitler's Army*, p. 84.
77. Sajer, *Forgotten Soldier*, pp. 118–19.
78. Quoted in Ernst Klee, Willi Dressen, and

Volker Riess, eds., *"The Good Old Days"*: *The Holocaust as Seen by Its Perpetrators and Bystanders.* New York: Konecky and Konecky, 1991, pp. 83–84.

79. Quoted in Klee, Dressen, and Riess, *"The Good Old Days,"* pp. 81–82.

80. Quoted in Klee, Dressen, and Riess, *"The Good Old Days,"* p. 78.

## Chapter 6: "Stand and Die": The Defense of the Fatherland

81. Quoted in Stephen E. Ambrose, *D-Day, June 6, 1944: The Climactic Battle of World War II.* New York: Simon and Schuster, 1994, p. 36.

82. Quoted in Ambrose, *D-Day*, p. 518.

83. Ambrose, *D-Day*, p. 577.

84. Quoted in Paul Carell, *Invasion—They're Coming!: The German Account of the Allied Landings and the 80 Days' Battle for France.* New York: E. P. Dutton, 1963, p. 59.

85. Samuel W. Mitcham Jr., *The Desert Fox in Normandy.* Westport, CT: Praeger, 1997, p. 85.

86. Carell, *Invasion—They're Coming!*, p. 60.

87. Quoted in Ambrose, *D-Day*, p. 452.

88. Quoted in Martin Blumenson and the Editors of Time-Life Books, *Liberation.* Alexandria, VA: Time-Life Books, 1978, p. 17.

89. Quoted in Blumenson, *Liberation*, p. 59.

90. Quoted in Cornelius Ryan, *The Longest Day.* New York: Simon and Schuster, 1959, p. 263.

91. Ryan, *The Longest Day*, p. 263.

92. Quoted in Cornelius Ryan, *A Bridge Too Far.* New York: Simon and Schuster, 1974, p. 327.

93. Quoted in Ryan, *A Bridge Too Far*, p. 327.

94. Quoted in Ryan, *A Bridge Too Far*, p. 328.

95. Luck, *Panzer Commander*, p. 149.

96. Knappe and Brusaw, *Soldat*, p. 23.

97. Knappe and Brusaw, *Soldat*, p. 60.

98. Stahlberg, *Bounden Duty*, p. 399.

99. Knappe and Brusaw, *Soldat*, p. 338.

## Epilogue: Aftermath

100. Otto Friedrich, *Before the Deluge.* New York: Harper and Row, 1972, p. 11.

101. Bernt Engelmann, *In Hitler's Germany: Daily Life in the Third Reich.* New York: Pantheon, 1986, pp. ix–x.

102. Knappe, *Soldat*, pp. 338–39.

103. Quoted in Dan Bar-On, *Legacy of Silence: Encounters with Children of the Third Reich.* Cambridge, MA: Harvard University Press, 1989, p. 281.

104. Quoted in Alison Owings, *Frauen: German Women Recall the Third Reich.* New Brunswick, NJ: Rutgers University Press, 1993, pp. 100–101.

# For Further Reading

David Fraser, *Knight's Cross: A Life of Field Marshal Erwin Rommel*. New York: HarperCollins, 1993. This biography of Rommel offers the definitive study of the celebrated field marshal's life and death.

Daniel Jonah Goldhagen, *Hitler's Willing Executioners*. New York: Vintage Books, 1996. This controversial book examines the involvement of ordinary German citizens in the Holocaust.

William K. Goolrick, Ogden Tanner, and the Editors of Time-Life Books, *The Battle of the Bulge*. Alexandria, VA: Time-Life Books, 1979. Cowritten by a veteran of the Battle of the Bulge, this book contains hundreds of vivid photographs.

John Keegan, *The Second World War*. New York: Penguin Books, 1989. This comprehensive history covers each theater of the war, beginning with the successes of blitzkrieg and ending with the defeat of Japan.

———, *Six Armies in Normandy*. New York: Viking Press, 1982. This book covers the events that took place in Normandy from D day to the liberation of Paris.

Volkmar Kühn, *Rommel in the Desert: Victories and Defeat of the Afrika-Korps, 1941–1943*. West Chester, PA: Schiffer, 1991. Originally published in German, this book gives details about the desert campaigns waged by the Afrika Korps under Rommel.

William W. Lace, *The Nazis*. San Diego: Lucent Books, 1998. The history of the Nazi movement in Germany from 1919 through World War II.

Russell Miller, *Nothing Less than Victory*. New York: William Morrow, 1993. Compiled from letters, diaries, official reports, and interviews with veterans of both sides, this book tells the story of those who took part in D day.

Earle Rice Jr., *The Final Solution*. San Diego: Lucent Books, 1998. This book covers the origins, development, and implementation of the Final Solution.

———, *Nazi War Criminals*. San Diego: Lucent Books, 1998. This book looks at six major Nazi war criminals and the roles they played in the Final Solution.

Cornelius Ryan, *The Last Battle*. New York: Simon and Schuster, 1966. The author conducted hundreds of interviews with Americans, Germans, and Russians for this chronicle of the fall of Berlin.

Anne Grenn Saldinger, *Life in a Nazi Concentration Camp*. San Diego: Lucent Books, 2000. This book provides an in-depth look at conditions in Nazi concentration camps.

Gerald Simons, *Victory in Europe*. Alexandria, VA: Time-Life Books, 1982. This volume in Time-Life's World War II series details the fall of Nazi Germany.

Gail B. Stewart, *Hitler's Reich*. San Diego: Lucent Books, 1994. Hitler's rise to power and the conditions in Germany during the Nazi era.

John Toland, *The Last 100 Days*. New York: Random House, 1965. This reconstruction of the last one hundred days of World War II in Europe is based on more than six hundred interviews with veterans of both sides of the war.

# Works Consulted

Christopher Ailsby, *SS: Hell on the Eastern Front: The Waffen-SS War in Russia, 1941–1945*. Osceola, WI: MBI, 1998. This book contains numerous black-and-white photographs showing the *Waffen-SS* in action on the eastern front.

Stephen E. Ambrose, *D-Day, June 6, 1944: The Climactic Battle of World War II*. New York: Simon and Schuster, 1994. Based on information from government and private archives, and from American, British, Canadian, French, and German veterans, this massive work chronicles the events of D day.

Dan Bar-On, *Legacy of Silence: Encounters with Children of the Third Reich*. Cambridge, MA: Harvard University Press, 1989. The author interviewed the children of people who were involved in the Third Reich.

Omer Bartov, *Hitler's Army: Soldiers, Nazis, and War in the Third Reich*. New York: Oxford University Press, 1992. The author challenges the view that Wehrmacht soldiers were not adherents of Nazi Party ideology.

Martin Blumenson and the Editors of Time-Life Books, *Liberation*. Alexandria, VA: Time-Life Books, 1978. A title in Time-Life Books' World War II series, this book covers the events of the liberation of France.

Richard Breitman, *Official Secrets: What the Nazis Planned, What the British and Americans Knew*. New York: Hill and Wang, 1998. Breitman reviews Nazi atrocities and details when and how news of them reached the Allies.

Paul Carell, *Invasion—They're Coming!: The German Account of the Allied Landings and the 80 Days' Battle for France*. New York: E. P. Dutton, 1963. This book contains German accounts of the Allied invasion of Europe.

Claire Chevrillon, *Code Name Christiane Clouet: A Woman in the French Resistance*. College Station: Texas A&M University Press, 1995. Written by a French woman who went into hiding in Paris to escape the Gestapo, this book details the French resistance to the German occupation of World War II.

Richard Collier and the Editors of Time-Life Books, *The War in the Desert*. Alexandria, VA: Time-Life Books, 1977. A comprehensive view of the battles and conditions in North Africa during World War II.

Robert Crowley and Geoffrey Parker, eds., *The Reader's Companion to Military History*. Boston: Houghton Mifflin, 1996. This reference book contains 570 articles covering battles waged by Western powers.

Franklin M. Davis Jr. and the Editors of Time-Life Books, *Across the Rhine*. Alexandria, VA: Time-Life Books, 1980. This book covers the Allies' crossing of the Rhine River and their drive into the heart of the Third Reich.

Len Deighton, *Blitzkrieg: From the Rise of Hitler to the Fall of Dunkirk*. New York: Ballantine, 1982. An analysis of the strategy, tactics, and machines of the blitzkrieg and the men who carried out the campaigns in Poland and western Europe.

Bernt Engelmann, *In Hitler's Germany: Daily Life in the Third Reich*. New York:

Pantheon, 1986. This book describes how ordinary German citizens lived during the Nazi era.

Otto Friedrich, *Before the Deluge*. New York: Harper and Row, 1972. This book focuses on Berlin in the 1920s, before the Nazi takeover of Germany.

Stephen G. Fritz, *Frontsoldaten: The German Soldier in World War II*. Lexington: University Press of Kentucky, 1995. This book about German infantrymen in World War II contains numerous excerpts from letters, diaries, and memoirs.

Donald M. Goldstein, Katherine V. Dillon, and J. Michael Wenger, *Nuts!: The Battle of the Bulge*. Washington, DC: Brassey's, 1994. Commemorating the fiftieth anniversary of the Battle of the Bulge, this book is an extensive collection of photographs from one of the most critical engagements of World War II.

Heinz Guderian, *Achtung-Panzer!: The Development of Armoured Forces, Their Tactics, and Operational Potential*. 1937. Reprinted London: Arms and Armour, 1992. This book lays down Guderian's theories of tank warfare.

———, *Panzer Leader*. New York: Da Capo, 1996. Guderian's autobiography gives vivid portraits of the leading personalities of the Third Reich.

Hamburg Institute for Social Research, *The German Army and Genocide: Crimes Against War Prisoners, Jews, and Other Civilians in the East, 1939–1944*. New York: New Press, 1999. A catalog of evidence of criminal activities on the part of the Wehrmacht.

Ernst Klee, Willi Dressen, and Volker Riess, eds., *"The Good Old Days": The Holocaust as Seen by Its Perpetrators and Bystanders*. New York: Konecky and Konecky, 1991. An extensive collection of excerpts from diaries, letters, and interrogations of Nazi war criminals, along with many photographs they and others took of their atrocities.

Siegfried Knappe and Ted Brusaw, *Soldat*. New York: Dell, 1992. Based on Knappe's wartime diaries, this memoir delves into the life of a soldier in Hitler's army.

Ronald Lewin, *The Life and Death of the Afrika Korps*. New York: Quadrangle/The New York Times, 1977. The story of the Afrika Korps from its inception to final defeat.

James Lucas, *Hitler's Enforcers*. London: Arms and Armour, 1996. A military historian focuses on Wehrmacht commanders of Nazi Germany.

———, *War on the Eastern Front*. London: Cooper and Lucas, 1991. A history of German soldiers in Russia from the German point of view.

Hans von Luck, *Panzer Commander: The Memoirs of Colonel Hans von Luck*. New York: Dell, 1989. Von Luck fought in every major German campaign during World War II.

John Lukacs, *Five Days in London: May 1940*. New Haven, CT: Yale University Press, 1999. The deliberations of Churchill and the British War Cabinet on the eve of the Dunkirk evacuation.

Kenneth Macksey, *Rommel: Battles and Campaigns*. New York: Mayflower, 1979. Lavishly illustrated, with maps and photographs, this book examines Rommel's military career from World War I through his death in 1944.

Samuel W. Mitcham Jr., *The Desert Fox in Normandy*. Westport, CT: Praeger, 1997. This book shows the legendary Desert Fox, Field Marshal Erwin Rommel, in action at Normandy and details the fighting during and immediately after D day.

Roderick de Normann, *For Führer and Fatherland: SS Murder and Mayhem in Wartime Britain.* Sutton, England: Phoenix Mill, 1996. This book examines the lives of *Waffen*-SS soldiers who went into captivity as prisoners of war in Britain.

Richard Overy and Andrew Wheatcroft, *The Road to War.* London: Macmillan, 1989. This book details the rebuilding of the German military between the world wars and the events that led to World War II.

Alison Owings, *Frauen: German Women Recall the Third Reich.* New Brunswick, NJ: Rutgers University Press, 1993. The author interviewed German women about their lives during the Nazi era.

Martin Pöppel, *Heaven and Hell: The War Diary of a German Paratrooper.* New York: Hippocrene Books, 1988. Pöppel fought in Norway, Crete, the Russian front, Italy, and Normandy, and ended the war in a POW camp in England.

David Pryce-Jones, *Paris in the Third Reich: A History of the German Occupation, 1940–1944.* New York: Holt, Rinehart and Winston, 1981. A history of the German occupation of Paris, with numerous photographs and personal interviews with both Germans and French.

*Reporting World War II: American Journalism: Part One, 1938–1944 and Part Two, 1944–1946.* New York: Library of America, 1995. This two-volume set includes dispatches from all theaters of the war by many famous as well as lesser-known American journalists.

Horst Fuchs Richardson and Dennis Showalter, eds., *Sieg Heil!: War Letters of Tank Gunner Karl Fuchs, 1937–1941.* Hamden, CT: Archon Books, 1987. Compiled, edited, and translated by Karl Fuchs's son, these personal letters give a startling glimpse into the mind of a young Nazi soldier.

Cornelius Ryan, *A Bridge Too Far.* New York: Simon and Schuster, 1974. This book details Operation Market Garden, the Allied plan to capture the bridge across the Rhine at Arnhem, which ended in defeat.

———, *The Longest Day.* New York: Simon and Schuster, 1959. The author personally interviewed seven hundred D day survivors from both sides in order to reconstruct the events of June 6, 1944.

Guy Sajer, *The Forgotten Soldier.* Washington, DC: Brassey's (US), 1990. This inside view of the Wehrmacht was written by a Frenchman who served in the German army.

Heinz Werner Schmidt, *With Rommel in the Desert.* New York: Ballantine, 1967. This firsthand account of the German campaign in North Africa is written by Rommel's aide-de-camp.

William L. Shirer, *The Rise and Fall of the Third Reich: A History of Nazi Germany.* New York: Simon and Schuster, 1960. Written by a distinguished American journalist who was based in Germany for many years, this is one of the first comprehensive histories of the Nazi era.

Gerald Simons and the Editors of Time-Life Books, *Victory in Europe.* Alexandria, VA: Time-Life Books, 1982. Part of Time-Life's World War II series, this book details the violent collapse of the Third Reich and the aftermath of the war in Germany.

Alexander Stahlberg, *Bounden Duty: The Memoirs of a German Officer, 1932–1945.* London: Brassey's (UK), 1990. Stahlberg fought in Poland, France, and Russia, and played a part in the July 20, 1944, attempt on Hitler's life.

Johannes Steinhoff, Peter Pechel, and Dennis Showalter, *Voices from The Third Reich: An Oral History.* New York: Da Capo,

1994. This book is drawn from dozens of interviews with Germans who lived through the Nazi era, some of them for-

brigadier general who fought against Rommel and was captured by him in North Africa.

Christian Zentner and Friedemann Bedürftig, eds., *The Encyclopedia of the Third Reich*. New York: Da Capo, 1997. This extensive reference contains more than three thousand entries pertaining to Nazi Germany.

# Index

Afrika Korps
  battles
    for El Alamein,
      51–52
    of Tobruk, 49–50
  desert conditions,
    45–46
  defense in Tunis,
    52–53
  food rations, 47
  leisure time, 46–47
  surrender to Allied
    forces, 53
  uniforms and equip-
    ment, 48
  use of tanks, 48–49
  waging war in the
    desert, 44–45
  wounded in action,
    50–51
air force (*Luftwaffe*), 8,
  15, 68, 73
air raids, 73–75
ambushes, 30
Ardennes Offensive,
  71–73
armaments, 48–49
Arnhem, Holland, 71
artillery barrages, 35–36
Atlantic Wall, 67

automatic assault rifles, 72
Barbarossa Jurisdictional
  Decree, 57
Bartov, Omer (historian),
  54–55, 58, 64
blitzkrieg strategy,
  15–16, 19
blizzards, 39
Böhme, Franz, 59
Breitman, Richard (his-
  torian), 61
Bulge, Battle of the,
  71–73

cannibalism, 39
Chevrillon, Claire, 27, 29
children, 28
civilians, 58–60
Cologne, Germany, 73
combat
  hand-to-hand, 71
Commissar Order, 43,
  57–58
comrades, 37
concentration camps, 59

D day
  Allied landings, 68

casualties and prison-
  ers, 69–71
fighting in the
  hedgerows, 68–69
final phase of war,
  66–67
Death's Head SS, 59
Deighton, Len, 14
desert campaign
  conditions during,
    45–46
  tanks and armaments,
    48–49
  uniforms and equip-
    ment, 48
  *see also* Afrika Korps
Desert Fox. *See* Rom-
  mel, Erwin
desertions, 43
Dietrich, Sepp, 62
diseases, 45–46

*Einsatzgruppen*, 61, 65
El Alamein, battle for,
  51–52
Engelmann, Bernt, 79
executions, 30, 43
  *see also* war crimes

Fatherland. *See* Germany, Nazi

firing squads, 63

food rations, 25, 47

fortifications, 67

France, invasion of, 19–21

   *see also* Normandy, France

France, occupation of

   contact with civilians, 27–28

   departure from Paris, 31

   fraternization, 28–29

   off-duty activities, 26–27

   resistance and retaliation, 29–30

   room and board, 25–26

   soldiers as tourists, 23–24

   training and waiting, 24–25

fraternization, 28–29

Fritz, Stephen (historian), 39, 42

Fuchs, Karl

   memoirs of, 19, 24, 55–56

furloughs, 27

Geneva Convention, 33, 54, 56

genocide, 55–57

Germany, Nazi

   aftermath of war, 78–81

   defense of Berlin, 73–75

   heroes of, 73

   program of genocide, 55–57

   rearmament of, 13–15

   strength and power, 11

   surrender of, 76–77

Greater Germany (*Grossdeutschland*), 9–10

Groth, Verena, 81

Guderian, Heinz, 15, 16, 19

guerrilla fighters, 29, 30, 58–59

Hague Convention, 33, 54, 56

Hansmann, Claus

   memoirs of, 34, 38, 41–42

Hartl, Albert, 65

historians, soldiers as, 64

Hitler, Adolf

   Commissar Order, 43, 57–58

   death of, 75–76

   failed assassination attempt, 70

   as leader of Germany, 11, 12

   orders to die fighting, 69

   in Paris, 26

Hitler Youth, 8

holidays, 19, 46–47

horse races, 27

hospitals, field, 41–42

hunger, 39

hunting, 27, 46

immigrants, German, 78–79

jaundice, 46

Jewish citizens, 30, 54, 56–57, 60

   *see also* war crimes

Kluge, P., 60–61

Knappe, Siegfried

   memoirs of, 18, 20, 25, 27, 35–37, 74–77, 80

leisure time, 19, 46–47

Lewin, Ronald, 44

Lucas, James (historian), 35

Luck, Hans von
    memoirs of, 15–17, 24,
        26, 73
*Luftwaffe* (air force), 8,
    68, 73

Macksey, Kenneth (his-
    torian), 50
Maquis, 30
marriage, 27
Mattera, James, 62
medical corps, 41
Mielert, Harry, 39
military training, 8–9,
    12–13, 24
minefields, 40
Montgomery, Bernard,
    51
Moscow, 33

National Socialist Ger-
    man Workers' Party, 12
National Socialist Lead-
    ership Officers, 54
Nazi Party organization,
    12, 43
Nazis
    ideology of, 10–11
    propaganda of, 9–10,
        54, 55

*Nebelwerfer* (rocket
    launcher), 35, 72
Normandy, France
    Atlantic Wall, 66–67
    beaches of, 68
    casualties on D day,
        69–71
    hedgerow country,
        68–69
North Africa. *See* desert
    campaign
Nuremberg trials, 56

occupied countries, 23,
    25, 29
    *see also* France, occu-
        pation of
off-duty activities, 26–27
opera and theater, 27
Operation Sea Lion, 24
Order Police (*Ordnung-
    polizei*), 8

Panzer I (tank), 14
Paris, 23–24, 31
partisan attacks, 58–60
Peiper, Joachim, 62
Polish campaign, 16–17
Pöppel, Martin, 24, 25,
    70
POWs

crimes against, 33, 62
German prisoners as,
    50, 52, 71, 78
ruthless brutality to-
    ward, 62–63
propaganda, 9–10, 54, 55
protection squads
    (*Schutztaffel*)
    membership in the,
        8–9
    role of, 60–62

race hatred, 56–57
    *see also* war crimes
restaurants and night-
    clubs, 27
Ringsdorff, Alfred, 71
Rommel, Erwin
    leader of Afrika Korps,
        15, 44–45
    retreat from El
        Alamein, 51–52
    Tunis defense, 52–53
room and board, 25–26
Russia, invasion of
    combat
        sound of, 34–36
        stress of, 40–41
    Commissar Order, 43,
        57–58
    early victories, 33–34
    eastern front, 32–33

effects of cold weather,
36–39
escalation in brutality,
42–43
final days of war, 43
Germany's defeats dur-
ing, 38–39
overwhelming force of,
39–40
Russian attacks during,
39–40
war crimes against
POWs, 32–33, 62–64
wounded in action,
41–42
Ryan, Cornelius, 69


Sajer, Guy
memoirs of, 35–36,
38–41, 62–63
sandstorms, 45
Schmidt, Heinz Werner
memoirs of, 46–47, 49,
50–51
Schumann, Karl, 37
Serbia, occupation of,
59–60
Shirer, William L., 26
Sitzkrieg period, 17–19
Slavic citizens, hatred
against, 55–57
see also war crimes

snowstorms, 38–39
Soviet Union. See Russia
SS (Schutztaffel)
crimes against POWs,
62
membership in the,
8–9
role of, 60–61
Stahlberg, Alexander, 15,
21, 75–76
Stalingrad, Battle of, 39
Stauffenberg, Schenk
von, 70
Streithofen, Basilius, 64
Suez Canal, 51



tanks, 14, 48
Sherman, 49, 69
Teuchert, Friedrich von,
31
Third Reich, 8, 75
see also Germany,
Nazi
Tobruk, Battle of, 49–50
Toland, John, 75
Treaty of Versailles, 10,
12, 35
Tunis defense, 52–53



uniforms and equip-
ment, 48

war crimes
Commissar Order, 43,
57–58
against humanity, 56
against Jews and Slavs,
54–57
partisan battles, 58–60
against POWs, 33,
62–65
stress of murder, 65
war criminals, 78
war reparations, 12
weather, 36–39
Wehrmacht (armed
forces)
Nazi ideology, 10–11
war crimes of, 33, 54,
57, 59, 62
winter
clothing, 37
conditions, 36–39
Woltersdorf, Hans, 10,
39
World War II
aftermath of, 78
battles
for El Alamein,
51–52
of the Bulge, 71–73
blitzkrieg strategy,
15–16
D day, 66–67

desert campaign,
44–45
invasion of
France, 19–21
Russia, 32–33, 57–58
Operation Barbarossa
(map), 32

Polish campaign,
16–17
preparing for, 13–15
the *Sitzkrieg*, 17–19
surrender of Germany,
76–77
Tunis defense, 52–53

wounded in action
desert campaign,
50–51
eastern front,41–42

Yugoslavia, occupation
of, 57

# Picture Credits

# About the Authors

Cherese Cartlidge and Charles Clark are freelance writers and editors who live in Georgia. Cherese attended New Mexico State University, where she received a B.A. in psychology. Charles attended New Mexico Highlands University and received degrees in philosophy and psychology. He and Cherese have been collaborating on writing and editing projects since 1998.